Pavlov

Jeffrey A. Gray

Fontana Paperbacks

First published by Fontana Paperbacks 1979
Copyright © Jeffrey A. Gray 1979

Set in Linotype Pilgrim

Made and printed in Great Britain by
William Collins Sons & Co. Ltd, Glasgow

A hardback edition of this book is published by
Harvester Press

To the memory of Dr A. H. Black

Contents

Abbreviations used for works cited
in the text are listed on page 139.

1. Intellectual Background

One of the greatest puzzles we face is how to understand the relations between behaviour, mind and the brain. No one has done more than Pavlov to bring this puzzle out of the realm of philosophy and into the laboratory. In doing so, he established a vital bridge between physiology and psychology, two subjects which were virtually isolated from each other when his career began, but are now almost at the point of fusion; and he converted the programmatic sketches of nineteenth-century philosophical materialism into an experimental science whose methods and results now deeply affect our lives. For these reasons, Pavlov is justly regarded as one of the founding fathers of modern experimental psychology; and his influence on contemporary views of Man and his place in the world has been correspondingly great. Yet he was neither a philosopher nor a psychologist: he was a physiologist who first achieved scientific eminence for research on the digestive glands. Only after this, at the age of fifty, did he develop the concept for which he is today remembered: the conditioned reflex.

The basic experiment in which Pavlov demonstrated the conditioned reflex is well known. A dog is prepared in such a way that it is possible to measure the amount of saliva secreted by its salivary glands. The dog is hungry and, when it is given a small piece of food to eat, it salivates copiously. Now the experimenter makes use of a 'stimulus' (e.g. a flashing light, a ticking metronome, or a steady tone) which, by itself, has no effect on the flow of saliva, and this is regularly 'paired' with the food. That is to say, the dog is regularly presented with, say, the flashing light and immediately afterwards with a piece of food. After the light and the food have been presented together a few times in this way, the light alone comes to produce a strong flow of saliva. It is this salivation in response to a stimulus which is initially ineffective ('neutral'), but which becomes effective in consequence of its association with food, that Pavlov called a 'conditioned reflex'.

Subjectively, of course, we all know the phenomenon: it is the 'watering of the mouth' which occurs in anticipation of eating. Bernard Shaw, as part of a diatribe against Pavlov in *Everybody's Political What's What*, gives an equally homely example of a conditioned reflex:

What, exactly, is a conditioned reflex? I became intellectually conscious of one some fifty years ago, when there was opened at Chelsea a Naval Exhibition. It contained facsimiles of Nelson's last flagship .and of the first class passengers' quarters in a modern Peninsular and Oriental Liner. I gazed without discomposure on the cockpit in which Nelson kissed Hardy and died. But in the passage between the P. and O. cabins I suddenly felt seasick, and had to beat a hasty retreat into the gardens. This was a perfect example of a conditioned reflex. I had often been made seasick by the rolling and pitching of a ship. The rolling and pitching had been accompanied by the sight of the passengers' quarters and the smell of paint and oakum. The connection between them had been so firmly established in me that even when I stood on the firm earth these sights and smells made me squeamish.

Pavlov's research on conditioned reflexes is considered in detail in Chapter 3. In this and the next chapter we shall first look at the background out of which this research grew.

Ivan Petrovich Pavlov was born in 1849, the eldest son of a poor parish priest of peasant stock, in the small Russian town of Ryazan, about 150 miles south-east of Moscow.

He started his formal education at the age of eleven in the Ryazan Ecclesiastical High School and went on from there to the local seminary. This does not seem a likely place to breed a mind destined to revolutionize European scientific thought. But the Russian seminaries, as it turned out, were the breeding ground for revolutionaries of many kinds. And, in the 1860s, under the relatively liberal regime of Czar Alexander II, it was possible for senior pupils to read what we would nowadays call 'progressive' magazines, finding in them the latest intellectual trends or scientific discoveries. We know from Pavlov's reminiscences that he was deeply affected by this 'literature of the sixties', and especially by the writer Pisarev, who popularized scientific thought while also acting as a propagandist for the radical political movement known as the 'Nihilists' (portrayed by Turgenev in his novel *Fathers and Sons*). It was through Pisarev's writings, for example, that Pavlov first became acquainted with Darwin's theory of evolution.

In his small-town church school, then, Pavlov was by no means cut off from the intellectual and scientific climate of his day. So it is worth stopping a moment to consider where European thought stood at that time on the great issues to which he was due shortly to make such a vital contribution.

The modern history of the mind-brain problem starts with Descartes (1596–1650). Descartes held that the body is a machine. Animals, having no souls, are automata; Man, however, has a soul, and it is the soul which perceives and wills. The soul and body interact in the pineal gland, situated at the base of the brain. (In case this be thought excessively antiquarian, bear in mind that the eminent physiologist, Sir John Eccles, proposed essentially the same idea in 1953; only now the soul is permitted to interact with nerve-cells all over the brain under the cover of the Heisenberg uncertainty principle.) It was left to the French materialists of the eighteenth century, La Mettrie and Cabanis, to go one step further and proclaim that Man, too, is but a machine, and that the brain secretes thought as the stomach secretes digestive juices.

It is one thing to proclaim a faith such as this, but quite another to work it out or show why it is to be preferred to others. Neither in Descartes' time nor in La Mettrie's was much known about how *l'homme machine* might actually work. The principles of reflex action were still to be worked out by the immature science of physiology. Since these principles were to be fundamental to Pavlov's thinking, it is worth tracing the major steps in their development.

The modern physiology of the nervous system rests on three critical and intertwined concepts. The first is structural : the nerve-cells or 'neurons' as the separate elements which make up the nervous system. The second is functional : the nervous impulse (an electrochemical wave propagated along the neuron) as the way in which information is transmitted by neurons. The third is part structural and part functional : the reflex arc as the simplest way in which neurons combine to transform an incoming event ('stimulus') into behaviour adapted to deal with that event ('response').

It was just after Descartes' death that Robert Hooke first saw a living cell in the microscope (1665). But it was not until the middle of the nineteenth century that microscopic methods progressed sufficiently for the fine structure of the nervous system to become visible. Only then was it realized that the long nerve fibres in the spinal cord (along which Descartes had supposed the 'animal spirits' to course to and from the brain) are each extensions of a corresponding cell-body. The anatomical observations of Deiters (1865) and Golgi (1885) established what we now know to be the basic features of the neuron (see Figure 1) : the cell-body, with its nucleus; one long and prominent extension of the cell-body in the form of an axis cylinder (now termed the 'axon'); and many finer extensions sprouting from the cell-body (often in the opposite direction to the axon), now called 'dendrites'. We know today that each such neuron is

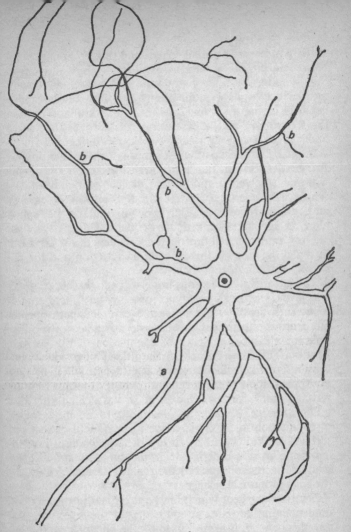

Figure 1. 'A large granular cell from the anterior horn of the spinal cord. × 300–400. In the cell substance is dark yellow pigment. *a.* is the chief axis-cylinder process. *b.b.b.* are fine axis-cylinder processes springing from protoplasmic processes. These latter are easily damaged and become difficult to see, whereas the chief axis-cylinder process *a.* resists destruction by reagents.'
From Deiters (1865).

spatially separate from all others, and that communication between them takes place across a small junction (termed the 'synapse' by Sherrington in 1897), which is usually located between the axon of the 'sending' neuron and a dendrite of the 'receiving' one. But the dominant view in the second half of the nineteenth century was that nerve fibres form a complicated network, or 'reticulum', interconnecting with each other in a maze of spatial continuity. The battle between the 'reticularists' and their opponents was not resolved until the first decade of the twentieth century. By this time, Pavlov was well into his researches on conditioned reflexes, and his own thinking was much more in keeping with reticularist ideas. This, as we shall see in Chapter 5, had profound consequences for the form in which he cast his theory of brain function and for the subsequent fate of that theory.

The nature of the nervous impulse, and whether or not it was even electrical, remained obscure until late in the nineteenth century. But in 1850 Helmholtz performed a momentous experiment in which he was able, for the first time, to measure the speed of conduction of the nervous impulse. This experiment entirely altered all previous conceptions of 'animal electricity'. It had been thought that the transmission of the nervous impulse was so fast as to be virtually unmeasurable. One estimate was as high as 57,600 million feet per second. Yet Helmholtz found the velocity of conduction in the frog's nerve to be a mere 90 feet per second. As Boring, in his *History of Experimental Psychology*, says of this experiment, it 'measured what had been ineffable, actually captured the essential agent of mind in the toils of natural science.'

The third concept which has been critical to the modern understanding of reflex action is that of the reflex arc. Today this concept is firmly based on the known structure of the neuron and the electrochemistry of nerve impulses and synaptic transmission. But the gross phenomenon of reflex movement has been known for centuries. Galen, in the second century of our era, had already described what we now call the pupillary reflex, that is, the automatic contraction of the pupil when the eye is exposed to bright light. The word 'reflex' was first used by Descartes and then developed by Astruc in 1736, who used it to mean simply a reflection, as in a mirror: 'as with light, angles of incidence and reflection are equal, so that a sensation produced by a concussion of the animal spirits against the fibrous columns (of the spinal cord) is reflected and causes motion in those nerve tubes which happen to be placed directly in the line of reflection.' Today, this optical analogy has been replaced by the electrochemical theory of nervous activity. But the basic notion has not changed much over two centuries: the action of the spinal cord in response to stimulation is automatic, and it depends on the spatial arrangement of incoming ('afferent') and outgoing ('efferent') nerve-fibres. A stimulus (say a prick to the skin) causes a train of impulses to pass along the afferent fibres to the spinal cord. There they cause a message to cross the synaptic junction. This in turn activates the efferent fibres, which give rise to a response (say a withdrawal of the limb to which the prick was applied). The nature of the response is determined by the interconnections in the spinal cord of afferent and efferent fibres. And the response (limb withdrawal) is adapted to the stimulus (the prick) because of these interconnections.

Anyone who has wrung a chicken's neck has seen spinal reflex action. That is to say, they have seen that the spinal cord can control integrated patterns of movement in the absence of the brain. More formal observations, entering this fact into the records of science, were reported by Robert Whytt in Edinburgh in 1751, though he used frogs. In the next century Marshall Hall (1790–1857) demonstrated in the spinal cord centres of nervous control (besides the bundles of nerves travelling to and from the brain which, in the dominant view of the time, were all that the cord contained). But, having shown that the cord can integrate reflex action on its own, without the brain, what inferences shall we draw about the locus of consciousness or mind? Shall we allocate these mysterious entities to the brain *and* the spinal cord, to the brain but *not* the spinal cord, or to neither? These questions were the subject of a heated debate during the middle of the nineteenth century.

This debate, difficult enough in its own right, was made worse by the fact that much of the discussion was in French or German. In neither of these languages do the key terms (*l'âme* and *die Seele*) make the invaluable English distinction between 'soul' and 'mind'. Thus the protagonists in the debate described the central issue as that of the existence, or otherwise, of a 'soul in the spinal cord', no less. In English, it is easier to keep psychology and physiology separate from theology. We shall find it safer, therefore, if less dramatic, to think of this question with 'mind' or 'consciousness' substituted for 'soul'; though there is no doubt that the actual course of the discussion over the years has been strongly influenced by theological considerations.

The out-and-out materialist answer to the question, 'where is the mind?', is 'nowhere'. But the first materialist move was to take mind away from the newly discovered centres of nervous control in the spinal cord. Whytt had drawn the opposite inference from his experiments on spinal reflexes: he had concluded that the mind might be everywhere in the body. At the same time, however, he emphasized the distinction between voluntary movements, said to be dependent on the brain and will, and involuntary movements, which were automatic and dependent on the spinal cord alone.

Hall, in the next century, agreed that spinal reflexes were involuntary and automatic, but added that they were independent of feeling or consciousness. Hall's view was in turn attacked by the German physiologist Pflüger (1829–1910), who argued that consciousness is a function of all nervous activity, in the cord as well as in the brain. If, he said, you divide the spinal cord of a cat into two parts, the cat acquires two 'souls'. Liddell, writing in 1960 about these beliefs of Pflüger, is scornful, as would have been the majority of twentieth-century scientists or philosophers. Yet, shortly after, exactly the same problem re-emerged in modern guise with reports of the 'split-brain' operation carried out in human beings for the treatment of epilepsy. In this operation, the commissures (bundles of nerve fibres) connecting the left and right halves of the brain are severed. It then turns out that the two halves of the brain can (under appropriate experimental conditions) each separately carry out very complex functions of which the other half apparently remains unaware. What do we now do? Do we say that there are 'two foci of consciousness' (the modern equivalent of 'two souls'); or treat one half of the brain (no doubt, the speechless one, normally on the right) as 'merely reflex', and the other as the only conscious one?

These issues are too important to be left to the ebb and flow of fashionable belief. Criteria are needed by which to distinguish the conscious from the unconscious. The controversy between Pflüger and Hall cast up some suggestions for such criteria. Pflüger defended his own position by pointing to the *purposeful* nature of spinal reflexes. After decapitation, a frog's leg will scratch the exact point where its skin is irritated by the application of acid. The philosopher Lotze countered by pointing out that, while reflexes are apparently purposeful in a normal environment, they do not adapt to changed circumstances. Consciousness, according to Lotze, enables action to go beyond reflexes by *adapting to change*. But it was then demonstrated by Auerbach that adaptation to change can occur in a decapitated frog. In this experiment, Auerbach amputated one of the frog's legs. If acid was now applied to the flank on the side of the missing leg, the remaining leg made only ineffectual efforts to remove the acid. Its reflex function was apparently confined to its own side of the body. Now, however, Auerbach made a slight change in the conditions of the experiment. He put a drop of acid on both sides of the frog's body.

The result was that the one remaining leg swung up and removed first the acid on its own side, and then the acid on the opposite side of the body. Here was good evidence for the capacity of a reflex to adapt to changed circumstances – the loss of one leg – provided the conditions were right.

These experiments, and the controversy in which they were embedded, set the stage for Pavlov. For the central thrust of the theory of *conditioned* reflexes was to explain how an animal adjusts to a changing environment. But conditioned reflexes were still half a century in the future. And it was not left for Pavlov to take the next step and treat the brain, as well as the spinal cord, as simply a centre for organizing reflexes. This step was taken by another Russian, Sechenov.

Pavlov later described the profound impression made on him by Sechenov's monograph, *Reflexes of the Brain* (1863). The title of this book was imposed by the censor (then as now a ubiquitous feature of Russian life), but it is pretty apt. The thorough-going materialist philosophy enunciated more than a century earlier by La Mettrie was now turned into a *physiological* theory. This was achieved by the simple expedient of treating all complex forms of behaviour as 'reflexes of the brain'. Thus emotional behaviour consists of reflexes whose intensity is augmented by the action of the brain; voluntary behaviour consists of chains of reflexes built up during early development as the result of 'absolutely involuntary learning'; and thoughts consist of reflexes whose motor expression is inhibited. As the final insult, Sechenov turned Pflüger's argument on its head and defined involuntary (i.e. *reflex*) movements as purposive. 'Involuntary movements are always expedient. By means of these movements the animal tries to prolong a pleasant sensory stimulation, or attempts to eliminate the stimulus by avoiding it.'

We now know, with the development of cybernetics and the engineering of control systems, that Sechenov's claim on this score was a reasonable one. But at the time it was a bold move, for it had as little foundation as the opposing claim made by Pflüger that purpose is the mark of soul. So much for the effort to find criteria for consciousness : it ended in assertion and counter-assertion, as, unfortunately, it still does today.

In truth, brilliant and wide-ranging as Sechenov's speculations were, there was little in them which stood on an empirical foundation. To the basic principles of spinal reflex action (themselves only at that time imperfectly understood) Sechenov could add only one key experimental discovery of his own. This was the observation that, by placing a crystal of salt on the cut (head) end of the spinal cord, it is possible to inhibit spinal reflex action. This demonstration that the brain could inhibit reflexes was the exiguous basis for the hypothesis that thought consists in inhibited reflexes. The empirical observations needed to turn Sechenov's outline into a full-bodied scientific theory were to be provided by Pavlov; though he was to use quite different methods from those used by Sechenov – methods that we would today call psychological rather than physiological.

The notion of the reflex was to be central to Pavlov's thinking, as it was to Sechenov's, and as it has been to the whole of modern physiology. And there is much in Sechenov's work which prefigures Pavlov's discoveries, notably the idea that complex behaviour may arise from the *learning* of reflexes, and the central role played by the concept of inhibition. But the recipe for Pavlov's work on conditioned reflexes required two further ingredients. The first of these was conceptual : the notion of association.

Other nations have gone in for grander metaphysics; but, as Boring remarks, British empiricist associationism 'is most peculiarly the philosophical parent of experimental psychology.' Again we must go back to the fecund seventeenth century to trace its beginning. First Hobbes (1588–1679) and then Locke (1632–1704) sought to refer the contents of the mind to the experience of the senses, and thus eliminate the innate ideas which Descartes favoured. Thus Locke asked: 'Whence has it [the mind] all the materials for reason and knowledge? To this I answer, in one word, from experience. In that all our knowledge is founded, and from that it ultimately derives itself.' This approach to the problem of knowledge required the *analysis* of the contents of the mind into elements (called by Locke 'ideas'), and some means for *combining* these elements into more complex structures. The doctrine of 'association of ideas' was meant by Locke, and by generations of his philosophical successors, to perform the latter task.

The different varieties of associationist theory may be defined by their 'laws of association', i.e. by the conditions which were said to be necessary for associations of ideas to take place. Both in the eighteenth century (Hume, Hartley) and in the nineteenth (James Mill, John Stuart Mill, Bain), the laws of contiguity (in time or space) and repetition commanded universal assent. Contiguity in time was intended to include both the simultaneous occurrence of two events or sensations and the case in which one immediately precedes the other. More in dispute was the law of resemblance: Hume thought that association of ideas can arise from their similarity, Hartley did not; and in the next century the same difference of opinion divided James Mill (against resemblance) from his son, John Stuart (for it).

In many ways, the theorist whose conclusions most clearly foreshadowed Pavlov's was David Hartley (1705–57), perhaps because he was a physician as well as a philosopher. Hartley was a psycho-physical dualist, that is, he believed that mental and physical events proceed along parallel lines, but do not interact. He believed that nervous activity involved vibrations of particles in the nerve fibres, and that within the brain there are 'diminutive vibrations, which may also be called Vibratiuncles and Miniatures'. As a dualist, it was necessary for him to state two sets of laws of association, one for the mind and one for the body. The one for the mind reads as follows: 'Any sensations A, B, C etc., by being associated with one another a sufficient Number of Times, get such a power over corresponding ideas, a, b, c etc., that any one of the Sensations A, when impressed alone, shall be able to excite in the Mind, b, c etc., the Ideas of the rest.' The parallel law for the body was identical, except that 'Vibration' was submitted for 'Sensation' and 'Miniature Vibration' for 'Idea'. To turn this into one of Pavlov's laws of conditioning, we need only perform a further substitution : 'stimulus' for 'sensation' and 'reflex' for 'idea'. And, just as Hartley postulated 'vibratiuncles', so Pavlov (as we shall see in Chapter 4) postulated activity in the cells of the brain.

Associationist philosophy reached its apogee in the mid-nineteenth century. It was a major influence on the new experimental psychology, which was officially born in Germany in the same year, 1860, that Pavlov started school in Ryazan. But Pavlov was not a philosopher. He did not advance associationist theory by pursuing further the armchair speculation which had spanned more than two centuries since the time of Hobbes and Locke. Instead, he turned speculation into knowledge by applying a new experimental method. This method was the final – and the critical – ingredient that would be necessary for associations to be transmuted into conditioned reflexes. It grew naturally out of Pavlov's first scientific researches. These were concerned, however, with other matters: the blood and the gut.

2. Physiological Researches

By the time Pavlov left the Ryazan Seminary to go to St Petersburg University in 1870 he was already set on a career in science. In his third year in the university he decided that this career was to be in physiology. He finished at the university in 1875 and went on to study medicine at the Medico-Surgical Academy, from which he graduated in 1879. He was already known as a promising research worker. Thus he was at once asked by Professor Botkin, director of the medical clinic at the Academy, to take charge of his newly opened laboratory for animal experiments.

Thereafter, Pavlov's history is the story of his experiments and the theories he built round them. The first part of that story was purely physiological. It lasted until the end of the century. By that time, Pavlov had completed the work for which he was awarded (in 1904) the first Nobel Prize ever given to a physiologist or to a Russian. Only after this did he commence his investigations of conditioned reflexes. But we can already see, in his research on the circulation of the blood and the functions of the digestive glands, the methods which would give his experiments on conditioned reflexes their profound impact.

Pavlov's first sustained series of experiments, covering roughly the period 1876–88, were concerned with blood pressure and with the innervation of the heart. Unlike his later work on the digestive system, they have had little lasting impact on physiology. Nonetheless, some of these early experiments already bear the hallmark of Pavlov's research : they rely on long-term, repeated observations in normal, unanaesthetized animals. Thus, when he wished to investigate the way in which blood vessels adapt to different volumes of blood, he trained dogs to lie absolutely still on

24

a table so that he could connect an artery to a pressure gauge. In this way he was able to measure blood pressure regularly and repeatedly in the same individuals (just as the family doctor does today, in unconscious imitation of Pavlov's initiative), and so demonstrate that it remains remarkably constant in spite of considerable differences in blood volume (induced by fasting, feeding or watering the animals).

This solution to the problem of measuring blood pressure was characteristic. Pavlov believed that it is impossible adequately to study or understand a single organ or function in isolation from the rest of the body. This point of view had just been eloquently expounded by the famous French physiologist, Claude Bernard, whose doctrine of *le milieu interne* was published in 1878. Bernard had written: *'Tous les mécanismes vitaux, quelque variés qu'ils soient, n'ont toujours qu'un but, celui de maintenir l'unité des conditions de la vie dans le milieu intérieur.'* ('All vital mechanisms, however varied they may be, have only ever one goal, that of maintaining the constancy of the conditions of life in the internal environment.') This doctrine, in its modern form, has become the theory of homeostasis; and, clothed in axioms taken over from engineering, it is fast on the way to becoming an impenetrable mathematical formalism. But the basic idea has remained the same: organisms are constructed in such a way as to maintain certain fundamental constancies in their internal environment.

The doctrine of *le milieu interne* determined the kind of experiment that Pavlov regarded as worth doing. He avoided the so-called 'acute' experiment, in which the animal is anaesthetized, the organ of interest is separated from the rest of the body, its function (to the extent that there still is one) is investigated as rapidly as possible, and the animal is killed when the experimenter has gleaned such information as he can. Pavlov used acute experiments on occasions, but only with great reluctance: 'when I dissect and destroy a living animal, I hear within myself a bitter reproach that with rough and blundering hand I am crushing an incomparable artistic mechanism.' (*B*, p. 162.) And he distrusted data obtained in this way because of the crude damage that is done to the integrity of the organism. Whenever possible he conducted instead 'chronic' experiments, in which the animal is conscious, healthy and available for repeated and careful observations. The experiment on blood pressure is a good example of this approach.

The blood pressure experiment required only a simple operation, taking a few minutes and involving a minute and painless cut through the skin. More elaborate surgery was necessary, however, to provide animals suitable for chronic experiments on the digestive system. This was the problem which occupied him for the last ten years of the nineteenth century, culminating in a book, *The Work of the Digestive Glands* (1897), which more or less established the science of gastro-enterology. Pavlov's chief interest in digestion was to elucidate the mechanisms determining the pattern of secretion of the different digestive juices (in the mouth, stomach, pancreas etc.) in response to meals. In a lively passage, he compares the action of the digestive system to

a chemical factory, where the raw materials – the foodstuffs – are submitted to an essentially chemical process. In this factory the foods are brought into a condition in which they are capable of being absorbed into the body fluids and made use of for the maintenance of the processes of life. The factory consists of a series of compartments, in each of which the food, according to its properties, is either retained for a time or at once sent on to the next; and each single compartment is provided with suitable reagents. These reagents are either prepared in adjoining little workshops, burrowed into the walls of the laboratory itself, or else in distant and separate organs, connected, as in other large chemical factories, with the main workshop by a system of transmitting tubes. (*WDG*, p. 2.)

In the analysis of the workings of this chemical factory, Pavlov's 'first problem', he tells us,

> consisted in the working out of a method. It was necessary to know how the reagents were poured out upon the food brought into the digestive factory. To accomplish this in an ideal manner required the fulfilment of many and difficult conditions. Thus it was necessary to be able to obtain the reagents *at all times*, otherwise important facts might escape us. They must be collected in *absolutely pure condition*, if we were to determine how their compositions varied, and also in *accurately measurable quantities*. Lastly, it was necessary that the *digestive canal should perform its functions normally*, and that the *animal under experiment should be in perfect health*. (*WDG*, pp. 3–4.)

It has been said that, in science, method is all. New facts and theories grow from methods which allow new observations to be made. This was certainly the case in Pavlov's research; and, in the passage just cited, he tells us exactly why he came to develop the methods which were to be so successful in the analysis, not only of the digestive system, but also in the later study of conditioned reflexes. But method does not necessarily mean technique. Often, and this again was so in Pavlov's case, the method itself is simple, and could have been put to use at any time. Pavlov was not the first person to train a dog to lie still. It was, rather, a new conception of the observations needed which led him to train a dog in this way for the purpose of a physiological experiment. It is here that we see that capacity to look at the fundamentals of a problem afresh that makes a great scientist.

When it came to the digestive system, however, Pavlov's

fresh perception of the problem, by itself, would have been insufficient. It was fortunate that he was also, as Sechenov said, the best surgeon in Europe. For, to carry through the programme he had set himself, it was necessary to get *inside* the digestive system, to the points where those 're-agents' were actually secreted into the digestive canal. This had been tried before, notably by the German physiologist Heidenhain, in whose laboratory in Breslau Pavlov had spent a short time. Heidenhain had brought out to the surface of the abdomen a part of the stomach and so formed a 'pouch' which remained connected to the rest of the stomach but had an opening directed towards the outside of the body. Pavlov made a critical modification in this pouch.

Heidenhain's pouch was prepared in such a way that practically all the nerves to the externalized stomach tissue were cut. Pavlov thought this might be the reason that the gastric secretion observed in a Heidenhain pouch is only very small in quantity. For he was convinced that most bodily functions are under the control of the nervous system. Indeed, the objective of his studies of the digestive system was to show that the secretion of the different digestive juices was controlled by a series of nervous reflexes similar to the motor reflexes of the spinal cord. Today the digestive tract would appear to be rather slippery ground on which to establish the action of the nervous system; for we know – as Pavlov did not – that a critical role in the control of the digestive juices is also played by hormones. But the first hormone was not discovered until 1902. And, by that time, Pavlov had demonstrated that there is indeed an important nervous regulation of the stomach and other intestinal organs. An important step in this demonstration was the conversion of Heidenhain's pouch into 'Pavlov's pouch', as it is still called in textbooks of physiology. This preserves intact the supply of nerves to the part of the stomach which opens out into the abdomen.

To make a Pavlov pouch requires great surgical skill. To

perform this operation, and others like it, Pavlov set up a special-purpose operating theatre for animals, the first in the world, and applied in it the new anti-septic methods developed by Lister and Pasteur. But it is important to see that the object of Pavlov's surgical methods was quite different from that of 'acute' surgery. The aim of the *chronic* surgical methods that he pioneered is to allow the experimenter to make observations while the animal continues to live *normally*, or at least as close to normally as possible. Most of the methods we use today to study the relations between physiology and behaviour stem directly from this Pavlovian tradition.

The stomach pouch was by no means Pavlov's only surgical innovation. He also developed, for example, a method which was later to be of critical importance for the study of conditioned reflexes. In this, part of the salivary glands is led out to the outside of the dog's mouth, permitting the study of saliva in the same way that the stomach pouch permits study of gastric secretions. In addition, he pioneered the technique of 'sham feeding' : an opening is made in the oesophagus, so that, when food is swallowed in the usual way, it falls out from the neck; the animal is fed by way of a second opening (a 'fistula') made in the stomach. In this way, it is possible to study how food placed in the mouth (but which never reaches the stomach) affects the flow of digestive juices in the stomach or other parts of the digestive canal. 'Sham feeding' has been extensively used since Pavlov's day in research on all aspects of eating.

Using these and other techniques Pavlov made the discoveries which won him the Nobel Prize. He demonstrated that the secretion of digestive juices in the stomach and the pancreas is controlled by the nervous system, and in particular by the vagus nerve. He showed that one consequence of this neural control is that the flow of both gastric and pancreatic secretions begins before any food reaches the stomach, and is initiated by the taste of food in the mouth. This 'psychic' secretion, as Pavlov called it, is of great importance for digestion. It can be by-passed in a dog with a gastric fistula by putting food directly into the stomach. When that is done, there is a flow of gastric juices caused by the presence of food in the stomach, but it is much less effective than the flow caused by normal feeding, and digestion correspondingly takes much longer. Thus 'psychic secretion' serves as a very effective 'appetite juice'.

The aptness of this phrase of Pavlov's was confirmed half a century later by Janowitz, who observed a woman patient with a gastric fistula. Janowitz found that the flow of gastric juices in his patient was much greater when she was presented with a meal she enjoyed rather than one she found dull and unappetizing. Thus Pavlov's insight that appetite is due in part to gastric juices reflexly elicited by pleasant food is also true of people.

While Pavlov's research on the digestive system has not had the enormous impact of his work on conditioned reflexes, it has nonetheless left an indelible impression on the science of gastro-enterology. Textbooks in this field still refer to his classic experiments, follow the lines he set down in posing the problems, and make use of the terminology he introduced. Yet for a while, beginning very shortly after the publication of *The Work of the Digestive Glands*, it seemed that his research might be eclipsed. The shadow which fell over it came from the discovery by Bayliss and Starling in London, in 1902, of the first hormone, secretin. This is liberated from the intestines during a meal and stimulates the secretion of pancreatic 'reagents', or enzymes, as we would now call them. This called into question the whole of Pavlov's reasoning; for he had attributed the release of pancreatic enzymes to purely neural influences and, in his experiments, he had failed to allow for the possibility of hormonal action.

The battle over these two opposing conceptions of the regulation of the digestive system, the neural and hormonal, aroused powerful echoes. For it was only in the second half of the nineteenth century that medicine had rid itself of he sterile doctrine of 'body humours' by which it had been dominated for over 2000 years. Virchow's ideas about cellular pathology and Pasteur's about bacteria had brought a new clarity in the understanding of disease; experiments in physiology were based increasingly on physics and chemistry; and the role of body humours in either health or disease had been thoroughly discredited. In the reaction against the humoral doctrine physiologists attributed an overwhelming importance to the nervous system. Even the nutrition of the tissues was thought by some, including Pavlov, to be under nervous control. Pavlov's allegiance to the concept of neural control was total. He expressed this in the doctrine of 'nervism', by which he understood 'a physiological theory which tries to prove that the nervous system controls the greatest possible number of bodily activities.' (*B*, p. 225.) Thus from Pavlov's point of view, Bayliss and Starling's ideas at first seemed like an attempt to put the clock back half a century.

Yet the evidence offered by Bayliss and Starling was incontrovertible. By cutting off a piece of intestinal tissue, making an extract of it in acid, and injecting this extract into the animal's jugular vein, they were able to provoke a strong pancreatic secretion. There could be nothing nervous about the action of such an extract. It had to be a 'chemical reflex' as the experimenters termed it. In today's language, it was the work of a hormone, that is, a substance which is liberated into the blood stream at one point in the body (in this case, the intestine) and changes the activity of an organ in another part (here, the pancreas). Thus was the ancient doctrine of the humours revived in modern guise. Pavlov accepted the truth of Bayliss and Starling's conclusions only when Savich repeated their experiments in his own laboratory. As Babkin describes the scene, after watching Savich's demonstration, Pavlov disappeared into his study without a word. He reappeared half an hour later and said : 'Of course, they are right. It is clear that we did not take out an exclusive patent for the discovery of truth.' (*B*, p. 229.)

Bayliss and Starling, for a while, seemed to believe that they *had* taken out such a patent. In a review paper in 1906 they dismissed altogether the possibility that the pancreas was under neural control. They too were finally convinced by experimental demonstration. Anrep, one of Pavlov's pupils, visited their laboratory in 1912 and showed them how stimulation of the vagal nerve causes the secretion of pancreatic juices. Thus, as is so often the case in major scientific controversies, both camps had part of the truth.

Today, in any case, the opposition between neural and hormonal theories is less stark. To thesis and antithesis there has now been added, in the approved Hegelian manner, a synthesis: the concept of the neuro-endocrine system. For in the last three decades it has become increasingly clear that the endocrine glands (i.e. those that produce hormones) are themselves controlled by the nervous system. Thus Pavlov's doctrine of nervism turns out to be right after all. But, before this synthesis was achieved, the battle between the neural and hormonal views of the digestive glands raged back and forth for another half-century; and, even today, many of the details of the interactions between nerves and hormones in the gut are unknown. Pavlov, however, was no longer in the fight. Partly because of Bayliss and Starling's work, his interests had turned elsewhere. 'Of course' he said to Babkin (*B*, p. 231), 'we may continue to study with success the physiology of digestion, but let other people do it. As for myself, I am getting more and more interested in the conditioned reflexes.'

3. Conditioned Reflexes

'Psychic secretion' was Pavlov's term for the gastric juices which pour forth in response to stimulation of the mouth by food. To reach the conditioned reflex we need to move one step away from the mouth and use stimuli which act upon the animal from a distance (for example, the sight or sound of food). It is not a big step to take. But, if there is a divide between physiology and psychology, this step takes you across it. Pavlov was well aware of this. He hesitated for a long time before he finally devoted his full attention to conditioned reflexes, which he first noticed incidentally during his work on the digestive system. And, for a while, he sought advice from psychologists about how to cross the great divide. But finally he decided that the advice he was getting from psychologists was not worth much; that the divide between physiology and psychology was illusory anyway; and that it was up to physiologists to study conditioned reflexes and, indeed, the whole of psychology.

Before describing this new phase in Pavlov's work, let us look at the psychology that he rejected. In 1900 experimental psychology was about forty years old, but still suffering the pains of a lengthy adolescence. It had become 'experimental' in about 1860, but, like most adolescents, it was still largely preoccupied with the inner life. In short, it was profoundly dualist. For some, this dualism took its original Cartesian form, mind and brain being separate but interacting (though the pineal gland was no longer in favour as the site of interaction). Others had been impressed by Helmholtz's theory of the conservation of energy (1847), and did not see how interactions between a material system and the spirit could take place without loss or addition of energy to the material system. But, rather than give up the

33

duality of body and spirit, they espoused the 'psychophysical parallelism' proposed by the German philosopher Leibnitz (1646–1716). According to this view, mind and body run on pre-ordained parallel courses, and the resultant correlations between mind-events and brain-events merely *appear* as though one might have caused the other. Either view allowed one to make a sharp distinction between psychology and the physical sciences. This distinction was also made by those who, philosophically, would not have regarded themselves particularly as dualists. This *methodological* dualism reigned supreme; and nearly all psychologists, especially in continental Europe, held that their proper subject of study was consciousness, and their proper method of study introspection.

To be sure, there were contrary trends. These were most pronounced in England and the United States, where the same impact that Sechenov and Pavlov had felt from Darwin was preparing the ground for behaviourism. Sechenov had seen almost as soon as *The Origin of Species* was published that the new evolutionary doctrine implied that mind had evolved; and that it could only have done so if natural selection acted on the physical organ of mind, that is, the brain, and on the functions discharged by mind, that is, behaviour. That same perception was clear to Darwin himself, to whom we owe the first explicit working out of a true comparative psychology (comparative, that is, between animals and Man) in *The Expression of the Emotions in Man and Animals* (1872). Thereafter the study of animal behaviour slowly began to gather speed, as did efforts to couch the results of this study in an objective language.

By 1900, when Pavlov's investigations of conditioned reflexes were just under way, these efforts had reached a critical point. In England, Lloyd Morgan had just (1894) formulated what came to be known as 'Lloyd Morgan's canon': 'in no case may we interpret an action as the outcome of the exercise of a higher psychical faculty, if it can be interpreted as the outcome of the exercise of one which stands lower in the psychological scale.' In Germany, Loeb had just (1890) developed his theory of tropisms, according to which the behaviour of at least lower organisms can be fully understood in physico-chemical terms; and Beer, Bethe and von Uexküll, in a paper cited approvingly by Pavlov, had just (1899) proposed that *all* psychological terms (like sensation, memory, learning) be discarded in favour of terms applying to changes in the animal's brain and body. And in America, Thorndike had just (1898) published his research on the way in which cats learn to get out of puzzle-boxes by clawing down ropes, pushing up bobbins, or combinations of these and other tricks.

So, in 1900, the battle between the 'objective' approach to psychology and the prevailing dualist orthodoxy was in full swing. The dualists consented to the establishment of laboratories for the study of animal behaviour. But they established the rule that, when you have finished making your observations of behaviour, you must use your results to infer the nature of the animal's conscious processes. To do this, you should put yourself in the animal's place and imagine what it feels like (just as you must if you wish to infer what goes on in the consciousness of another human being). So J. B. Watson, soon to become famous (or notorious, according to taste) as the standard-bearer of behaviourism, in a 1907 paper on the behaviour of rats still felt compelled to draw inferences about what the rat feels when it runs in a maze. The behaviourist revolution would be announced in 1913 when Watson overcame that compulsion, and proposed that behaviour was *all* one could study, in rat or Man.

In much the same way, Pavlov recounts how he struggled with a psychologically minded colleague during the first years of his work on conditioned reflexes:

I began to investigate the question of psychic secretion with my collaborators, Drs Wolfson and Snarsky. Wolfson collected new and important facts for this subject;

Snarsky, on the other hand, undertook to analyse the internal mechanism of the stimulation from the subjective point of view, i.e. he assumed that the internal world of the dog – the thoughts, feelings, and desires – is analogous to ours. We were now brought face to face with a situation which had no precedent in our laboratory. In our explanation of this internal world we diverged along two opposite paths. New experiments did not bring us into agreement nor produce conclusive results, and this in spite of the usual laboratory custom, according to which new experiments undertaken by mutual consent are generally decisive. Snarsky clung to his subjective explanation of the phenomena, but I, putting aside fantasy and seeing the scientific barrenness of such a solution, began to seek for another exit from this difficult position. After persistent deliberation, after a considerable mental conflict, I decided finally, in regard to the so-called psychical stimulation, to remain in the role of a pure physiologist, i.e. of an objective external observer and experimenter, having to do exclusively with external phenomena and their relations. I attacked this problem with a new co-worker, Dr Tolochinov, and from this beginning there followed a series of investigations with my highly esteemed collaborators, which has lasted for more than twenty years. (*G* I, pp. 38–9.)

Thus did Pavlov answer the question posed by Sechenov more than thirty years previously: who must investigate the problems of psychology and how? And his answers were the same as Sechenov's: physiologists, and by studying reflexes. His opinion of psychology and psychologists is often given in his papers, and it is invariably scathing. Psychologists of a later era have not repaid him in kind: having a good opinion of ourselves and our subject, we do him the highest honour by treating him as one of our most illustrious forebears. But Pavlov always regarded himself as a physiologist, though he had to invent a new branch of physiology in which to install his research. He called it the 'physiology of higher nervous activity', and this title continues in use today in the Soviet Union and in those parts of Eastern Europe which have come under strong Soviet – and therefore Pavlovian – influence. We thus have the somewhat odd situation that experiments which are done by psychologists in the United States and Western Europe are carried out by physiologists in Eastern Europe. There is perhaps no better illustration of the artificiality of the boundaries which separate one part of science from another.

At any rate, as he tells us in the passage just cited, Pavlov spent the rest of his life studying conditioned reflexes without further recourse to speculation concerning the inner life of his dogs. By the time he died, he had created a vast body of knowledge about conditioned reflexes and had organized it into a systematic theory of learning. A summary of his major findings still provides an accurate representation of much of what is known today about 'associative learning', as psychologists have come to call the field that Pavlov called 'the physiology of higher nervous activity'. The remainder of this chapter is devoted to such a summary. We shall leave theoretical interpretations of Pavlov's findings until the next chapter.

Pavlov used almost exclusively the salivary reflex. As we saw in the last chapter, the dog used in this kind of experiment first undergoes a minor operation in which part of the salivary flow is directed to a fistula protruding out of the mouth. The amount of salivation can now be recorded as the number of drops of saliva falling through the fistula. But it is important to realize that Pavlov's choice of the salivary reflex, and indeed of the dog, as his object of study was essentially arbitrary. Pavlov reckoned himself to be studying the *general* laws of 'higher nervous activity' (*sc.* behaviour) applicable in any higher organism and to any reflex. The dog's salivary reflex simply provided him with a handy method of investigating these laws. Later work has entirely justified his confidence in this approach. The principles he established have been shown to hold from earthworm to Man and over a wide range of different forms of behaviour. There is a good parallel between Pavlov and Mendel in this respect. Just as Mendel's work on the sweetpea established principles of genetics which are of almost universal application, in spite of the enormous apparent diversity of the living world, so did Pavlov's work on the salivary reflex establish general laws of learning.

The choice of the salivary reflex, then, was arbitrary; but it was not random. Pavlov already knew that it was experimentally convenient, that dogs made good experimental subjects, and that he could work if necessary for years with the same animal once it had been trained to stand still in the special harness he had constructed for his experiments. And he also knew a great deal about the *unconditioned* salivary reflex, that is, the flow of saliva which is provoked by food or other substances placed in the dog's mouth.

Before Pavlov's own experiments it had been believed that salivation is an undifferentiated response to any stimulation of the mouth, capable of varying in quantity only. Pavlov had demonstrated that this view was false. He showed that the *quality* of saliva (i.e. its chemical constitution) varies depending on the exact nature of the substance introduced into the mouth : different kinds of food release different kinds of saliva, and acid and other injurious substances release different kinds again. He made similar observations on the digestive juices in the stomach, and showed also that the co-ordination between salivary and gastric secretions depends on the substance ingested : food, for example, provokes both salivary and gastric secretions, acid only the former. All these finding were interpreted by Pavlov as evidence of the profound *purposiveness* of the unconditioned reflexes of the digestive glands. Thus, food in the mouth provokes the secretion of both saliva and gastric juices, because the saliva is preparing the food for its sub-sequent journey to the next stage in the 'chemical factory'; but acid in the mouth provokes the secretion of saliva only, because the purpose of this secretion is to expel the acid from the mouth, not to expedite its journey to the stomach.

An earlier age would have regarded such observations as evidence for a purposeful creation. But Pavlov came after Sechenov, and Sechenov after Darwin, so now signs of pur-pose had become evidence of the power of natural selection and the activity of the nervous system. Thus the salivary reflex offered Pavlov a delicately tuned instrument with which he could demonstrate, first, the way in which evolu-tion had adapted the species to its normal environment (the unconditioned reflexes); and, second, the way in which learning adapts individuals to the oddities of their own particular environments (the conditioned reflexes).

The transition to this second object of study had already begun when Pavlov wrote *The Work of the Digestive Glands*. He describes his first encounters with it as follows:

> In the course of our experiments, we found that all the phenomena of adaptation which we saw in the salivary glands under *physiological* conditions, such as the introduction of stimulating substances into the buccal cavity [the mouth], appeared in exactly the same manner under what we may call *psychological* condi-tions. That is to say, when we merely drew the animal's attention to given substances agreeable or disagreeable, or, when we offered it particular foods, a secretion either immediately appeared, or did not appear, in accordance with the previously ascertained effects of the substances when directly brought into the buccal cavity. (*WDG*, p. 83.)

The distinction between conditioned and unconditioned salivary reflexes may be drawn in three related ways. First, unconditioned salivation is produced by direct stimulation of the mouth; conditioned salivation is produced by stimulation of the so-called 'distance receptors' (the nose, eyes or ears). Second, and more fundamental, unconditioned salivation is produced by stimuli which are almost always connected with the nutritious qualities of food (or the injurious qualities of acid); conditioned salivation is produced by stimuli which are only accidentally connected with food or acid. Third, and most fundamental, unconditioned salivation is innate, a response built into the species by natural selection; conditioned salivation arises when an animal connects a stimulus with food or acid because of its own particular experience. The third distinction is possible only because of the second : it is the invariable connection between, say, a burning sensation and the injurious effect of acid in the mouth that provides natural selection with the materials out of which to build an unconditioned reflex beneficial to organisms which possess it. The first distinction is of limited significance. It happens that, in the case of salivation, the stimuli which evoke the unconditioned response must be applied to the surface of the mouth, and those which are used to evoke the conditioned response usually fall upon distance receptors. But there is no general need for this to be so : other unconditioned responses may be produced by distant stimuli (light eliciting the pupillary reflex is an example), and stimuli applied to the surface of the body may serve as conditioned stimuli.

Pavlov was already aware of these points when he wrote *The Work of the Digestive Glands*. He comments there on the great variety of stimuli which, because of the animal's particular experiences, may come to evoke salivation: 'Even conditions altogether collateral to the stimulus, such as the room and furniture of the room in which the animal is placed, the vessel containing the food, the presence of the attendant who ordinarily feeds the animal, the sound of his approach, produce an effect.' (*WDG*, p. 84.) Salivary reactions to furniture are clearly not the sort of thing that it is possible or profitable for natural selection to build into the design of a species. Each animal must learn that one for itself.

Thus did Pavlov discover the conditioned reflex (or rather, domesticate it into a scientific beast, for, like many things of importance, it has always been known). To study it, he needed something more manageable in the way of stimuli than the laboratory furniture. So he set up a number of pieces of apparatus to provide alternative sources of stimulation, ranging from lights, buzzers and bells, to metronomes, whirligigs and 'touchers', the latter being a device which could touch the dog at one or other point on its body. The first experiment to use these artificial stimuli was published in 1905, and thereafter they were in constant use. It soon became clear that the laws of conditioned reflexes have no respect for the stimulus used to produce them (or 'elicit' them, as the jargon has it): so long as the animal notices it, any stimulus will do. (Recent research, stemming from Garcia's work on bait shyness mentioned later in this chapter, has shown that this statement needs some qualification: under certain conditions, some stimuli may enter into association with each other more easily than others. But it remains generally true that the specific characteristics of the stimuli used in conditioning experiments have relatively small effects on the phenomena observed in them.)

We are now acquainted with the four key elements in a conditioning experiment and, since we shall need to refer to them time and again, it will be as well to introduce the standard terminology and abbreviations by which they are named. The 'unconditioned stimulus' (UCS) is the stimulus which has an innate capacity (i.e. without any special conditioning history) to elicit the response under investigation. In a typical salivary conditioning experiment it is a piece of food (meat, bread etc.) or a squirt of acid. The response to the UCS is the 'unconditioned response' (UCR), e.g. the saliva elicited by the food or acid. The 'conditioned stimulus' (CS) is a stimulus which at the start of the experiment does not elicit any salivation, but which (if the experiment is successful) comes to do so after it has been presented in association with the UCS. The 'conditioned response' (CR) is the response which is elicited by the CS after the experiment has been successfully carried out; in the salivary experiment, it takes the form of salivation. (Actually, Pavlov used the terms 'unconditional' and 'conditional', but the terms 'conditioned' and 'unconditioned', introduced by Anrep and Gantt in their translations of Pavlov, are now hallowed by use.) The process whereby the CS comes to acquire the power to produce the CR is called 'conditioning'.

These, then, are the bare bones of a conditioning experiment. Modern psychologists use such experiments as a window into the way in which animals form associations; and Pavlov too believed that he had brought the venerable associationist philosophy of Hume, Hartley and Mill into the laboratory. But there are dangers in this approach. In a conditioning experiment we measure the degree to which the animal's associations affect its behaviour. We can infer from the fact that a dog salivates to a bell that it has associated the bell with food. But the converse is not true: we cannot infer from the absence of salivation that the dog has *not* associated the bell with food. There may be other reasons (it may not be hungry, for example). Nor can we infer from the quantity of saliva exactly how strong is the association between bell and food; for the flow of saliva is affected by many other factors (for example, the dryness of the food). So a conditioning experiment provides at best a rather murky window into the dog's associations.

How to clear this window is an unsolved problem in contemporary psychology, and likely to remain so for some time to come. Thus it is safer to consider the generalizations which it has proved possible to draw from experiments on conditioning as empirical rules in their own right, at least in the first instance. These generalizations are based on a vast experimental literature (Razran in

1971 counted over 7000 conditioning experiments published in twenty-nine different languages). But their main lines have changed but little from those inferred by Pavlov himself.

The first two generalizations we can make concern the necessary conditions for the formation of a CR : (1) the CS and UCS must come into temporal contiguity; (2) they must do so repeatedly (though later we shall need to qualify both these statements). These generalizations parallel the two chief laws of association developed by Hume and his successors, those of contiguity and repetition. But, as is the way with empirical generalizations, they are both more precise and more complicated than the philosophical laws that they replace. In reaching an understanding of the complications, the reader may find it helpful during the following paragraphs to refer to Figure 2.

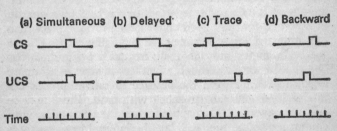

Figure 2. Schematic diagram of the temporal relationship between CS and UCS in (a) simultaneous; (b) delayed; (c) trace; and (d) backward conditioning.
From Mackintosh (1974).

To begin with, it turns out that, for the conditioned reflex, temporal contiguity is largely a one-way street. That is, the CS has to *precede* the UCS, if it is to acquire the capacity to elicit a response resembling the UCR. If the UCS (say, food) is presented before the CS (say, a bell), it is only under very special conditions that the bell comes to elicit salivation, and some authorities doubt that such 'backward conditioning' ever occurs at all. Pavlov himself remained in doubt on the matter; and his final view seems to have been that 'if the [conditioned] stimulus is introduced *after* the beginning [of the UCS], then, although ... a conditioned reflex may also develop, it is insignificant and evanescent.' (G I, p. 381.) Interestingly, only the most physiologically minded of the associationist philosophers, David Hartley, appears to have anticipated Pavlov's discovery that 'forward' conditioning is much more powerful than 'backward'.

Not even Hartley, however, had supposed that forward associations might be much more powerful than the simultaneous kind. Yet such is the case with conditioned reflexes. Neither Pavlov nor any of his successors has been able to demonstrate significant conditioning when the CS and UCS begin to act simultaneously. Yet it is sufficient for the beginning of the CS to precede that of the UCS by a quarter of a second for very good conditioning to take place; and the optimal interval between the beginning of the CS and the beginning of the UCS is, in the case of some reflexes, only half a second (though for others it may be a minute or so). Thus the nervous system treats temporal precedence in a radically different manner from simultaneity.

If we now ask what happens when the CS is allowed to commence before the UCS, but the interval between these two events is lengthened, quite a complex picture emerges. First, it is clear that animals can form conditioned reflexes when very long delays separate the onset of the CS from that of the UCS. Pavlov reported that conditioning could occur with delays of several minutes, provided the CS continued to act until the onset of the UCS (a procedure known as 'delay conditioning'). But if the CS comes to an end some time before the onset of the UCS ('trace conditioning'), it is much harder to form conditioned reflexes and they are unstable once formed. Nonetheless, even under these circumstances, conditioned reflexes may be established. Pavlov demonstrated them with trace intervals of up to two or three minutes. Later work has provided a particularly dramatic example of trace conditioning over a much greater interval. This is the so-called 'bait shyness' experiment, first reported by Garcia in the United States in 1966. The animal is fed a perfectly harmless, but distinctively flavoured substance and then, several *hours* later, it is exposed to some treatment which makes it feel sick. When subsequently offered food or drink flavoured in the same way, the animal resolutely refuses it. This is an unusual result (though perfectly reproducible), and psychologists are still working out the exact conditions on which it depends. But it establishes that, at least in some circumstances, a CS can be associated with a UCS from which it is separated by several hours.

Turning from contiguity to repetition, it has been shown with many different reflexes that the CR gradually strengthens as the pairing of CS with UCS is repeated. The strengthening of the CS may be measured as an increase in its probability of occurrence, in the speed with which it follows the CS, or in its size (for example, the number of drops of saliva). The number of pairings (or 'trials') needed for the CR to attain its maximum strength varies considerably depending on the reflex studied, the intensity of the stimuli used as CS and UCS, and many other factors. Occasionally, maximum reflex strength, or something very near it, is attained after only one pairing, and 'one-trial learning' is said to result. The bait shyness experiment is an example of this very rapid learning. In other cases, some hundreds of trials are needed before the CR becomes large and stable.

The factors which affect the size of conditioned reflexes were intensively studied in Pavlov's laboratory. Not surprisingly, if the function of the CR is to prepare the animal to adapt successfully to the expected UCS (which was how Pavlov thought of the matter), its magnitude normally varies in direct proportion to the magnitude of the UCS.

Thus a dog given a large portion of food as UCS salivates more to the CS than a dog given a small portion. It is also no surprise that a hungry dog displays more conditioned salivation than a sated one. Less obviously adaptive, though well established, is the observation that the size of the CR is usually directly proportional to the intensity of the CS. Thus a dog salivates more to a loud bell or a bright light that signals food than to a soft bell or a dim light. Since the animal is going to need the same amount of saliva to digest the food, however it is signalled, it is difficult to see any adaptive value in this 'law of strength', as Pavlov called it. As we shall see in Chapter 6, this law played an important part in Pavlov's theory of personality.

Another problem to which Pavlov devoted much attention is that of the 'generalization' of conditioned reflexes. Suppose you establish a CR using as CS a tone of a given pitch, loudness, duration etc. To what feature of the CS does the animal respond? Will it continue to respond if some of these features are changed? To answer these questions Pavlov made use of 'transfer' tests : after the animal has been trained with a particular CS–UCS combination, a different stimulus, never itself paired with the UCS, is presented, and the response it elicits is measured. He found that a stimulus tested in this way would often elicit a CR of the same kind as that elicited by the training CS, though usually smaller in magnitude. He further established that the size of this 'generalized' response is proportional to the similarity between the training CS and the test stimulus. If, say, the training CS is auditory and the test stimulus is visual, generalization will be less (i.e. the CR smaller) than if the test stimulus is also auditory. And if the established CS and the test stimulus are both auditory, but differ in, say, pitch, the size of the generalized response will be less, the greater the difference in pitch.

These observations are of the highest importance, for they open the way to a quantitative investigation of the perceptual world of animals. By constructing graphs relating the amount of generalized salivation to the characteristics of the stimuli used (distance from the CS in pitch, loudness, brightness, hue etc.) we can map the extent to which the animal perceives stimuli to be the same or different. Pavlov was quick to realize the power of this method of investigating perception in animals; and numerous investigations of this kind were carried out in his laboratory.

So much for the formation of conditioned reflexes. But much of Pavlov's research was concerned with their *disappearance*. From the start of his work in this field, he emphasized the fact that, unlike the UCR, conditioned reflexes very easily fade away; and he put much effort into understanding how and why this happens. In his successive explanations (for there were many) he invented a number of processes of 'inhibition' charged with the task of eliminating conditioned reflexes temporarily or permanently. We shall look at the progress he made in these efforts at explanation in the next chapter. For the moment I shall simply recount the major facts that he needed to explain.

In his final systematic exposition of these facts Pavlov divided them into two major classes. One of these he attributed to the operation of a process called 'external inhibition', the other to the operation of 'internal inhibition'. Internal inhibition covers those cases in which the CR disappears because the predictive relationship between CS and UCS is changed; in external inhibition, the predictive relationship between CS and UCS remains the same, but something else is altered in the experimental situation.

The simplest example of external inhibition is the disruption of a CR caused by any unusual or unexpected change in the animal's general environment, a sudden noise, say, or a change in the lighting of the experimental room. Pavlov sometimes waxes quite eloquent about the way in which the behaviour of his dogs was disturbed by

every sound, be it ever so small, appearing in the midst

of habitual sounds and noises which surround the dog, each weakening or reinforcement of these constant sounds, each change in the intensity of the room illumination (the sun becoming hidden by the clouds, a sunbeam suddenly breaking through, a flickering of the electric lamp, a shadow across the window), the appearance of a new odour in the room, a warm or cold current of air, something touching the skin of the dog, as a fly or a falling speck of plaster from the ceiling. (*G* I, pp. 133–4.)

Evidently, these unpredictable changes in his experimental set-up gave him a lot of trouble in his attempts to study conditioned reflexes systematically. Finally, in order to get rid of them, he built the world's first controlled environment specially constructed for the study of behaviour, equipped with sound-proof rooms and other devices to minimize interference between one experiment and another.

But the disruption caused in his experiments by such extraneous stimuli did not remain merely a nuisance for Pavlov. Characteristically, he set out to study it properly. He showed that any novel stimuli will disrupt ('inhibit') a conditioned reflex if it is presented to the animal simultaneously with, or just before, the CS. If, however, the novel stimulus is repeated a few times, it rapidly loses its disruptive capacity. On the occasions when it does inhibit conditioned reflexes, it can clearly be seen to attract the animal's attention: the dog may turn its head and eyes towards the stimulus, prick up its ears and so on. Pavlov described this attentive behaviour as the 'investigatory' or 'orienting' reflex. Subsequently, the orienting reflex became an important topic of research in its own right, especially in E. N. Sokolov's laboratory in Moscow. Experiments studying it have taught us much about attentive behaviour in both animals and Man.

The disruptive effects of novel stimuli which Pavlov described as 'external inhibition' are relatively easy to summarize. The changes which he grouped as 'internal inhibition' are more complex. He distinguished four subclasses of this type of inhibition: extinction, conditioned inhibition, differentiation and inhibition of delay. In each of them the predictive relationship between the UCS and other stimuli in the animal's environment is changed.

The simplest sub-class is extinction. In this, the experimenter stops following the CS by the UCS. In consequence, the CR (previously established to the CS) gradually weakens from trial to trial as the CS is presented alone. From this basic observation Pavlov concluded that the occurrence of the UCS is necessary to maintain the power of the CS to elicit a CR, an inference that he expressed by saying that the UCS 'reinforces' the CR.

Notice that the time course of extinction (and of the other varieties of Pavlov's internal inhibition) is quite different from that of external inhibition. When a novel stimulus is used, the disruption it causes in conditioned reflexes is maximal the first time it is presented to the animal, and the stimulus gradually loses its effectiveness with further presentations. When the UCS is omitted during extinction, in contrast, the CR is at first little affected and only gradually weakens over a number of trials. Thus graphs of the strength of the CR over trials in the two procedures are virtual mirror images of each other.

Another procedure which Pavlov classified as internal inhibition is known as 'conditioned inhibition'. This involves a third stimulus, besides the CS and UCS. This new stimulus (called a 'conditioned inhibitor') is presented together with the CS (usually, but not necessarily, just preceding it) and the combination is not followed by the UCS; on other interspersed trials the experimenter continues to present the CS unaccompanied by the conditioned inhibitor and followed, as originally, by the UCS. Thus the conditioned inhibitor predicts that the CS will not be followed by the UCS, whereas the CS on its own still predicts the occurrence of the UCS. The animal duly learns these relationships: the CR continues to be seen when the CS occurs on its own, but gradually disappears in response to the combination of CS and conditioned inhibitor. Furthermore, if the conditioned inhibitor is now presented to the animal in combination with a different CS, capable of eliciting the same kind of CR as the first CS, it disrupts the response also to the second CS. Thus the conditioned inhibitor acquires a general capacity to inhibit conditioned reflexes of the appropriate kind.

A third procedure involving inhibition was termed by Pavlov 'differentiation', though in contemporary texts the word 'discrimination' is often preferred. As in conditioned inhibition, a third stimulus is used, besides the CS and UCS. This 'differential stimulus' is never paired with either of the other two stimuli. At first, it acts simply like a novel stimulus, not eliciting a CR and, indeed, disrupting the CRs elicited by established CSs (external inhibition). With a few repeated presentations, however, the differential stimulus loses its power to act in this way and comes instead to elicit, by generalization, the same kind of CR as the established CSs. But if we continue to present the differential stimulus without following it by the UCS, the animal gradually ceases to respond to it once more. In other words, the generalized response to the differential stimulus disappears, just as in simple extinction the response to the original CS disappears.

As we saw earlier, generalization tells you which stimuli the animal spontaneously treats as similar. But it does not tell you what it can perceive as different. Differentiation gives you the other side of the coin. If the animal is able to respond to the CS with a CR, and inhibit the CR to the differential stimulus, it follows that it perceives the two stimuli to be different. Pavlov recognized the significance of differential conditioning as a tool to investigate the perceptual world of his dogs, and he used it for that purpose in many studies. In one of them, for example, he showed that a dog could perceive the difference between a circle and an ellipse even when the axes of the latter were in the ratio 9 : 8.

In this way, then, Pavlov began the scientific study, not only of associative learning, but also of perception in animals. Subsequently, an even more powerful method of studying the latter problem was developed, but this too grew out of observations initially made by Pavlov. This method, worked out in detail by Sokolov's group in Moscow, relies on the gradual disappearance of the orienting reflex with repetition of the stimulus eliciting it. The disappearance of the orienting reflex is known as 'habituation'. After habituation is complete, a slight change in the stimulus is sufficient to give it the power once again to elicit an orienting reflex. It follows, therefore, that the animal must have noticed the change. This method for studying fine sensory discriminations is much simpler than the conditioning method, since no preliminary training is required. Furthermore, it turns out to be far more sensitive : that is, fine differences to which the animal would find it difficult if not impossible to respond differentially in a conditioning experiment rapidly give rise to a return of the habituated orienting reflex.

Experiments on conditioned reflexes have made still other contributions to research on perceptual processes. Several phenomena first described by Pavlov have recently come to play a prominent role in theories of attention. Among these, for example, is an observation made during experiments on compound conditioning. In this kind of experiment the CS is made up of two components, e.g. a visual and a tactile stimulus, applied to the animal simultaneously. After conditioning to the compound CS is established, we test the animal's responses to the two components each presented separately. In such an experiment Pavlov noted that the response to one of the components tended to be 'overshadowed' by the other; that is, the response to the overshadowed component was less than it would have been, if it had been the only stimulus to which conditioning had been carried out. Thus the strength of conditioning to one component in a compound stimulus is critically dependent on the simultaneous presentation of the other component. Recent evidence suggests that the animal has, as it were, a limit to its capacity for conditioning. This may be thought of as a limitation on the degree to which it can attend to more than one stimulus at a time; or, alternatively, as a limitation on the degree to which it can at one time form associations between several CSs and one UCS. The more it devotes that capacity to one stimulus, the less it can learn about other stimuli. Thus, in a compound conditioning experiment, the stronger the CR which develops to one component of the compound, the less is the CR which develops to the other.

A further way in which conditioning experiments have opened up the study of animal perception concerns that most obscure sensory dimension, time. The sense of temporal duration is central to the final sub-variety of Pavlov's class of internal inhibitions: inhibition of delay. If a CR is first established with a relatively short interval between CS onset and UCS onset, and then this interval is increased, there is a gradual change in the timing of the CR. At first, it continues to make its appearance shortly after CS onset. With repeated experience of the new CS–UCS interval, however, the CR is gradually delayed until it occurs just before the onset of the UCS. On the assumption that the purpose of the CR is to enable the animal better to cope with the UCS (by, for example, ingesting it), this delay is clearly adaptive. Pavlov supposed that it involves the development of an inhibitory process (i.e. internal inhibition) during the early period after CS onset. Whether this inference is correct or not, it is clearly necessary for the animal to be able in some way to measure the passage of time so that the CR coincides with the occurrence of the UCS. Using the salivary reflex Pavlov reported successful delayed conditioning with CS–UCS intervals of up to three minutes.

Another method showed that dogs can measure periods of time ten times greater than this. The animal in this experiment was simply given a small piece of food every thirty minutes, with no preceding CS. Thus only the passage of time could act as a signal that food was about to come. Sure enough, Pavlov reports that the dog began to salivate about thirty seconds before the half-hour was up, thus displaying a capacity to measure even these long periods of time to an accuracy of just a few per cent.

Such is the power of method. For thousands of years people have speculated about the mental life of animals, about their powers to learn, see, hear or measure the passage of time. Suddenly, a simple new method made all these questions amenable to precise investigation and accurate solution. This method depended only tangentially on technical advances, such as the surgical procedure for bringing out the salivary gland to the surface of the dog's cheek. For the method of conditioned reflexes is quite general. All that is necessary is that the animal be exposed to regular sequences of stimuli, and that the experimenter observe the changed reactions which develop as a result of the predictive relationships which hold between these stimuli. But it is essential that these observations be made in a rigorously controlled environment, in which virtually everything that happens to the animal is determined by the experimenter. It was therefore no accident that Pavlov, during the course of his experiments on conditioning, found that he needed to construct a totally new laboratory to provide these conditions.

The need for such an artificial laboratory environment has made people question the relevance of conditioning experiments to 'real life'. But this is to misunderstand the purpose of experimental research. Conditioning experiments are not designed to discover how a dog salivates in response to a metronome ticking at 120 beats a minute, a typical stimulus used by Pavlov but not one that dogs often come across unless they live in extremely musical homes. They are designed, like most scientific experiments, to uncover the *general principles* which underlie the particular phenomena observed in any one set of circumstances. If it is possible to abstract these principles, they will be applicable in all circumstances (or they are not general enough, and we must return to the laboratory). In this way Mendel established principles of genetics in the sweet-pea which have proved to be applicable to the whole of the vegetable and animal kingdoms; and Pavlov established principles of learning and perception which have proved to be of almost equal generality, vegetables apart.

Another objection sometimes made to conditioning experiments is that they do not apply to Man; or, if they do, they apply only to trivial aspects of his behaviour. Put in the first form, this objection is certainly false. There have been many demonstrations of conditioning with human subjects, including, for example, the conditioning of salivation, knee-jerks, eye-blinks, the electrical resistance of the skin, the electrical activity of the brain and so on. Put in the second form, the objection is probably false; but in the absence of clear criteria of triviality, and with our still very imperfect knowledge of complex human behaviour, it is not possible to reject it out of hand. But there have been clear demonstrations of human conditioning working at a level which it is not easy to regard as trivial. Razran, for example, has described experiments on 'semantic' conditioning, in which it has been shown that, if a meaningful word is used as a CS, there is generalization of the conditioned response to other words, or even whole phrases, with the same meaning; and if a meaningful word is used as the UCS, aspects of its meaning are taken on by the CS. This kind of observation would not have surprised the associationist philosophers. And perhaps one guarantee that Pavlov's experiments are not wholly unrelated to the human mind is the fact that these philosophers deduced the same general principles from their own mental life as he did from the dog's saliva.

In that case, one final objection could run, why bother to study dogs at all? What has Pavlov told us that Hume, Hartley or Mill did not? To this there are many answers.

First, what Pavlov told us is known in a much more precise form than philosophical speculation can provide.

Second, the experimental method enables one to decide between rival views in a way that unaided introspection cannot. Only Hartley among the associationists, for example, thought that associations are formed in a forward direction, but not backward. Conditioning experiments support this view for, as we have seen, backward conditioning, if it occurs at all, is very fragile. And none of the associationists thought there might be a radical difference between simultaneous and successive associations; yet successive pairing produces conditioned reflexes and simultaneous pairing does not. There may be, of course, other ways of forming or studying associations to which these limitations do not apply; and, indeed, there are other experimental paradigms in which it is already known that backward associations may be formed. But this difference between experimental paradigms itself raises new problems which associationist philosophy could not, alone, have brought to light: namely, why do predominantly forward associations affect some kinds of behaviour and more general associations, others; and which forms of behaviour belong in the first category, and which in the second?

Yet a third reason for studying animals experimentally is that we can tackle problems which are amenable neither to armchair speculation nor to experimental investigation in Man. Take for example the question of internal sensations. To what stimuli are our internal organs sensitive? To what aspects of the function of these organs do we respond when we report rumblings in the stomach, chills in the heart and so on? It would take a brood of introspectionist psychologists, of the kind which filled the universities of Germany and Austria when Pavlov began working on conditioned reflexes, thousands of man-hours to classify (or fail to classify) these sensations; and they would still have no way of deciding what causes them. But, using the methods of conditioned reflexes and cunning devices to apply touches, temperatures, pressures or chemicals to the linings of the internal organs, Bykov in the Soviet Union and Adam in Hungary have made much progress in resolving these problems. Indeed the inner life of the dog is in some respects better known to us today than the inner life of Man.

The fourth and final answer to the question, what can we glean from conditioned reflexes that was not in the books of associationist philosophy, is an extension of the third. We can use them to study the brain itself. It is possible to apply the CS or UCS, or even both, to selected regions of the brain (stimulating them electrically, for example), and thus investigate directly the way in which the brain forms associations between two events. Such experiments could not be done in Pavlov's time, for the techniques of electrical stimulation and recording in the brain were not yet sufficiently advanced. But they have been carried out by later investigators; and research along these lines continues vigorously today.

But there is another sense in which the study of conditioned reflexes is in any case the study of the brain. This is certainly how Pavlov thought of the matter: the subtitle of his book *Conditioned Reflexes* is 'an investigation of the physiological activity of the cerebral cortex'. In the next two chapters we shall see what he meant by this.

4. The Theory of Conditioning

Pavlov's method of conditioned reflexes provides an un-rivalled tool for the collection of accurate information about the way in which associations (or at least certain kinds of association) are formed and broken. But science does not stop with the collection of facts. Its thrust is always towards theory. This thrust can take two forms. One can seek for the simplest set of unifying principles from which it is possible to deduce all the particular facts. Or one can invent an underlying mechanism so constructed that the particular facts can be deduced from its rules of operation. These two kinds of theory building are not mutually exclusive. Often, the two go hand in hand; and sometimes it is difficult to say whether a particular theory is of one kind or the other. Nonetheless, in the extreme, they are recognizably distinct. An example of the first kind is Newton's law of gravitation; an example of the second is Niels Bohr's planetary model of the atom.

Pavlov's account of conditioned reflexes contains both kinds of theory, and in a rather thorough tangle at that. Nonetheless, it is helpful to separate the two as far as possible. For their subsequent histories have been very different. We therefore deal in this chapter with the search for unifying principles among the varied data of condition-ing experiments; we shall leave until the next chapter the search for a mechanism underlying both principles and data.

The search for unifying principles is troubled by an issue which arises in virtually all behavioural experiments. The experimenter arranges that certain things shall happen to the animal; then he looks to see how the animal's behaviour changes. He hopes to attribute what he sees the animal do to what he does to the animal. The trouble is that what he does to the animal is usually open to more than one interpretation, and the animal's interpretation of what is going on may not coincide with the experimenter's. This difficulty worms its way to the very heart of any stimulus-response psychology. For both fundamental terms in the scientist's vocabulary, 'stimulus' (S) and 'response' (R), are Janus-like: we can consider them either from the experimenter's point of view or from the animal's.

From the experimenter's point of view, the 'S' in S–R psychology may be defined as any change in the animal's environment which can be shown to be related to a subsequent change in the animal's behaviour; and the 'R', as any change in the animal's behaviour which can be shown to be related to a prior change in its environment. But, from the animal's point of view (and this is what, in the end, it is the scientist's business to understand), the 'S' is the stimulus as the animal actually *perceives* it, and the 'R' is (in learning experiments) the response that the animal has actually learned to perform. We can present to an animal a flash of light whose characteristics (brightness, hue, duration, location etc.) can be precisely specified in physical terms (the experimenter's S); but only very prolonged experiments can determine how the animal perceives and classifies this stimulus (does he notice how bright it is, what colour it is etc.?). Similarly, our apparatus may record the flexion of a dog's paw (the experimenter's R); but equally prolonged experiments are needed to determine what the animal is trying to do with this movement (remove its leg from a particular place, move its body to some other place, feel a change in the tension of its muscles etc.). In short, 'S' can refer either to what the experimenter does or to what the animal observes; and 'R' can refer either to what the experimenter observes or to what the animal does.

The 'objective' terminology of conditioned reflexes (which Pavlov frequently stressed as one of the advantages of his approach) was in part an attempt to overcome these difficulties. But, once it has been accepted that reflexes are purposive (and, as we have seen, Pavlov not only accepted this, but treated it almost as a defining characteristic of reflexes), it becomes necessary to ask of a particular reflex, what *is* its purpose? Does a dog salivate to expel acid from its mouth, to dilute it, to prevent it from reaching the stomach, to make it taste less unpleasant? These are questions which Pavlov not only asked, but to which he suggested answers. To make matters worse, all these questions can be asked at two levels, which are often confounded. One can ask, what is the evolutionary history of a given reflex, i.e. in what way has it served the survival of the species? Or one can ask, what is the mechanism which produces the reflex in a particular individual, i.e. by what signs does the nervous system recognize that the reflex has been carried through to completion? The most obvious case in which these two kinds of answer diverge is that of sexual behaviour: at the evolutionary level, the purpose of sexual behaviour is procreation; at the individual level, it is the attainment of certain bodily sensations. Much ink has flowed in the cause of keeping these two 'purposes' together.

Thus the problem of analysing how the *animal* perceives and responds to the experimenter's carefully laid plans is not overcome by either the method or the terminology of conditioned reflexes; and much ink has flowed over this issue too. The questions which have come up are these:

1. What are the conditions which give rise to the formation of CRs?
2. What is the nature of the association formed in a conditioning experiment?
3. What are the conditions which give rise to the disappearance of CRs?
4. What is the nature of the process which causes the

disappearance of CRs?

The answers to these four questions define the first level at which one can approach the task of constructing a theory of conditioned reflexes, the level I have called 'the search for unifying principles'. Since Pavlov's time many different positions have been taken on all of them. I shall consider here only Pavlov's answers, and how they have stood up to later research.

The basic operation involved in a conditioning experiment is to present a CS which is followed shortly after by a UCS, and to repeat this on a number of occasions. Pavlov thought of this operation as providing the animal with repeated experiences of 'temporal contiguity' between CS and UCS (i.e. opportunities to observe the fact that the action of the UCS commences shortly after the action of the CS); and he regarded this temporal contiguity as the essential ingredient giving rise to a conditioned reflex. This then, in a nutshell, was his answer to the first of the four questions enumerated above: it stresses the relationship between CS and UCS as determining the formation of conditioned reflexes; and it describes that relationship as one of temporal contiguity.

Subsequent research and theoretical criticism have challenged both halves of this point of view. One attack on Pavlov's position has claimed that the important relationship determining conditioning is not between CS and UCS, but between the CR itself and the UCS. A second attack, while accepting that the important relationship is indeed between CS and UCS, rejects the description of this relationship as temporal contiguity.

It is impossible to deal adequately with the first attack on Pavlov's position without describing the other major tradition (besides that of conditioned reflexes) which has formed the modern theory of learning. This tradition deals with 'instrumental' or 'operant' conditioning. (These two words are synonymous. It is usual nowadays to distinguish

he method of conditioned reflexes from instrumental conditioning by calling the former 'classical' or 'Pavlovian'
conditioning.)

The basic procedure in a Pavlovian experiment, as we
have seen, is that the experimenter determines the sequenc-
ing of two stimuli, the CS and UCS, *irrespective of the
animal's behaviour*. In an instrumental conditioning procedure, in contrast, the experimenter specifies a relationship
between the animal's *responses* and a stimulus. For example, he may arrange for a rat to obtain a piece of food
if it runs to the end of an alley; for a pigeon to obtain
water if it pecks at a disc; or for a cat to escape from a box
by pulling on a rope.

It is clear that the basic procedures of classical and instrumental conditioning experiments are quite different.
Nonetheless, the two methods were inextricably confused
with each other for close on half a century; workers in the
two traditions used the same terms for quite different procedures or observations; and, not surprisingly, they usually
misunderstood each other.

Light first dawned in Warsaw, perhaps because of its
geographical position. Konorski and Miller had been trained
in the Pavlovian tradition (Konorski, indeed, by Pavlov
himself), but were sufficiently well acquainted with American experimental psychology to realize that the Americans,
while using the Pavlovian vocabulary (introduced into
America by Watson as the language of behaviourism), were
doing something quite different from Pavlov. Their now
famous paper, published in 1928, was the first to draw a
clear distinction between what they called Type I (classical)
and Type II (instrumental) conditioning. Subsequently, in
1935, the American psychologist B. F. Skinner drew the
same distinction, calling the two types 'respondent' (classical) and 'operant'. Even so, it was probably not until the
1960s that the procedural differences between classical and
instrumental conditioning were fully clarified.

The establishment of clear demarcations between the

procedures of classical and instrumental conditioning is one thing; but it is quite another to determine whether these different procedures give rise to different forms of learning or not. In this issue there have been – and still are – as many opinions as it is logically possible to hold. According to some theorists, there is only one kind of learning, and this is identical to the one described by Pavlov; on this view, instrumental learning is a disguised form of classical conditioning. According to others, there is only one kind of learning, and this is the one which occurs in an instrumental learning paradigm; on this view, classical conditioning is a disguised form of instrumental learning. Yet a third view holds that there is only one kind of learning, which cannot be identified either with classical or instrumental conditioning but underlies both. A final theory treats the two procedures as each engaging fundamentally different processes of learning.

The strongest attack on Pavlov's view that it is the relationship between CS and UCS which determines the formation of the CR has come from those who hold the second of the four views distinguished above, namely, that all learning is of the kind which is explicitly studied in an instrumental conditioning experiment (and, on this view, implicitly involved in a classical conditioning experiment). Theorists of this persuasion believe that all behaviour is learned because of its immediate consequences to the animal. The most powerful proponents of this belief have been some of Skinner's followers (though not Skinner himself).

These 'pan-instrumentalists', as we might call them, emphasize the importance in learning of the principle of reinforcement, sometimes known as the 'Law of Effect' (Thorndike's term). The term 'reinforcement' was first introduced by Pavlov, but he used it to mean the presentation of the UCS after the CS. As taken over by the pan-instrumentalists, 'reinforcement' means, roughly speaking, reward or punishment. Rewards are stimuli which increase the probability of recurrence of the behaviour which procures them; and punishments similarly decrease the probability of behaviour which they follow. This statement is Thorndike's Law of Effect. It is, of course, no law at all, but a definition of the terms 'reward' and 'punishment' (since we have no independent criterion for the correct use of these terms, besides the effects they produce on behaviour which they follow). Now, in a classical conditioning experiment, it is not obvious that any reward or punishment operates at all. At face value, in a conditioned salivation experiment, the animal does not salivate in advance of food *in order* to get food, but because it *expects* that food will occur anyway. Thus the task of the pan-instrumentalist is to find a hidden reward or punishment buried in this or any other classical conditioning procedure. We can then attribute the occurrence of the CR to the effects of such 'reinforcement'.

There are essentially two ways in which this move can be made. The first is to point out that, even though in fact the food (in a salivary conditioning experiment) is going to be presented to the dog whatever it does, the animal is ignorant of this part of the experimental plan. From the dog's point of view, each time it salivates, food follows. The probability of further salivation may therefore be strengthened in exactly the same way that the probability of bar-pressing is increased when food is procured *only* by pressing the bar. The second way is to argue that the food, to be sure, is presented irrespective of the animal's salivation, but the *effects* of the food are altered by this response (it may, for example, taste better or be easier to swallow). Thus the dog salivates in anticipation of the food *in order* to make it taste better, slide down more easily etc.

Innumerable experiments and theoretical arguments have been deployed over the years to support or refute these positions. This is not the place to enter into the details of the controversy. Many of the arguments have also been relevant to a second issue which we shall meet later in this chapter, namely Pavlov's 'stimulus substitution' theory of conditioning. We shall therefore postpone consideration of the relevant experimental material until we deal with this second issue; and even then we can give only the flavour of research in this field. Fortunately, this research has, in recent years, converged upon a solution of the problems at issue between those who have seen reward and punishment at work in classical conditioning experiments and those who (like Pavlov) have not. It is possible, therefore, to be dogmatic and brief.

Briefly, then, and dogmatically, Pavlov was right. The terms whose relationship determines the formation of a conditioned reflex are indeed the CS and the UCS, not the CR and the UCS. However, this is true only under certain conditions. Under other conditions it is the relationship between the animal's response and the reward or punishment which follows that response which determines its behaviour. Neither those theorists who wish to treat all learning as instrumental conditioning, nor those who wish to treat it all as classical conditioning, are correct. Both kinds of learning exist independently of each other. Or rather, they *can* be independent of each other under suitably purified experimental circumstances. Under most natural circumstances the behaviour of the animal is determined partly by each kind of learning process, sometimes co-operating with each other, but sometimes in conflict.

Thus, of the four possible positions one might logically hold on the issue of classical *versus* instrumental conditioning, only two are left tenable by the experimental evidence. The first is that there are two different learning processes, one which enables the animal to learn the relationships between stimulus events in its world (classical conditioning), and another which enables it to learn how to obtain what it needs and avoid what is harmful (instrumental conditioning). (This distinction is in some way like the philosopher's distinction between 'knowing that' and 'knowing how'.)

64

The second possibility is that there is a single learning process, more fundamental than either classical or instrumental conditioning and underlying both. This more fundamental process, however, if it exists, is so far rather nebulous; and it remains to be demonstrated how it would give rise to the sets of observations actually made in experiments on classical and instrumental conditioning.

So far, so good. Pavlov correctly identified the relationship between the occurrence of the CS and the occurrence of the UCS as the essential ingredient of a classical conditioning experiment. But was he right to describe this relationship as one of temporal contiguity? This is an issue about which there has been very little controversy. It has been rather generally assumed that temporal contiguity is indeed what matters in a CS–UCS pairing. But recent experiments have shown that the notion of temporal contiguity does scant justice to the complexity of the actual CS–UCS relationships to which conditioning is sensitive.

For the purpose of the discussion that follows it is necessary to distinguish between 'temporal contiguity' and 'contingency'. Consider a series of pairings of CS and UCS, with the CS each time slightly preceding and overlapping the onset of the UCS. On each occasion that the UCS starts to act there is temporal contiguity between CS and UCS. Temporal contiguity, in other words, is an event occurring at a particular point in time, though, of course, it may (and usually does) occur repeatedly. A contingency, in contrast, is a property of the whole series of pairings of CS and UCS. It is best defined in terms of two probabilities: (1) the probability that the UCS will occur, given that the CS has just occurred – symbolically, $p(UCS/CS)$; (2) the probability that the UCS will occur, given that the CS has not occurred – $p(UCS/\overline{CS})$, where $\overline{CS}$ stands for the absence of the CS. There is a positive contingency where the former probability is greater than the latter, i.e. where $p(UCS/CS) > p(UCS/\overline{CS})$. Both probabilities can only be

65

measured over a series of events consisting either of the paired presentation of CS and UCS or of presentations of the UCS alone. (There are similar arguments which apply to the case in which, as well as pairings of CS and UCS, there are presentations of the CS alone; but we shall not deal with them here.)

Now, if the UCS is never presented except after the CS, it is impossible to distinguish between contiguity and contingency. But as soon as we relax this rule (which Pavlov rarely did) the two concepts diverge. Consider, for example, an experiment using rats by the American psychologist, Rescorla. He divided an experimental session into units of time and varied the two probabilities identified above so that, in a given time unit, the probability that the UCS (an electric shock to the feet) would occur in the absence of the CS was either the same as or lower than the probability that it would occur in the presence of the CS. Let us take two particular conditions in the experiment. In both of them $p(UCS/CS) = 0.4$; that is, when the animal was presented with the CS, a shock UCS occurred four times in ten. In one of them, $p(UCS/\overline{CS})$ was set at this same value; in the other it was zero. Now, in both conditions, the animals had an identical number of experiences of temporal contiguity between CS and UCS, since $p(UCS/CS)$ was the same, 0.4. But in the condition in which $p(UCS/\overline{CS})$ was zero, the contingency between CS and UCS was substantial, since $p(UCS/CS)$ was greater than zero; while, in the condition in which $p(UCS/\overline{CS})$ was also set at 0.4, the contingency between CS and UCS was zero, since now $p(UCS/CS) = p(UCS/\overline{CS})$. It is clear that, if temporal contiguity between CS and UCS directly determines the degree of conditioning, then conditioning should have been equally good in the two conditions of Rescorla's experiment. The outcome of the experiment, however, was quite different. Substantial conditioning occurred in the condition in which no shocks occurred in the absence of the CS; no conditioning occurred at all when the probability of shock in the absence of the CS was identical to its probability in the presence of the CS.

We may capture the essential difference between the two conditions of Rescorla's experiment by saying that, in the one in which conditioning was successful, the CS conveyed information, namely, the information that shock was highly probable; while, in the other, it conveyed no information about shock that the rat did not possess already. In the former case, the CS *predicts* the UCS (albeit imperfectly); in the latter, it does not. There are other experiments which point to the same conclusion. Another American psychologist, Kamin, has described a phenomenon known as 'blocking'. To demonstrate this you need two groups of animals, two CSs (say a noise and a light), and a UCS (typically, electric shock). One ('control') group of animals receives pairings of a compound of tone-plus-light followed by shock, and is then tested for the magnitude of the CR to the light alone. The second ('experimental') group is treated in the same way, but before the compound conditioning trials it receives pairings of the noise CS with the shock UCS. The two groups receive equivalent amounts of experience of temporal contiguity between the light and the shock so that, if temporal contiguity were the all-in-all of conditioning, they should show equal CRs to the light when this is tested alone. In fact, Kamin showed that, although there was a substantial CR in the control group, the experimental group showed virtually no conditioning at all. Conditioning to the light, in other words, had been 'blocked' by the association that the animal had already formed between the noise and the shock. Notice that, as in Rescorla's experiment, conditioning failed to occur in that condition in which the light CS failed to predict anything about the occurrence of the UCS that was not already predicted by other factors in the experimental situation (in this case, by the noise CS).

These and other experiments, then, give rise to a rather different conception of the critical relationship between

CS and UCS which determines conditioning. This relationship is not (or not simply) one of contiguity, it is one of *prediction*. This idea would not strike Pavlov as strange. For he repeatedly stressed that a CS is a *signal* for the UCS. Thus, in the introduction to his only extended treatment of conditioned reflexes, he sets the scene for his new discoveries by writing :

> It is pretty evident that under natural conditions the normal animal must respond not only to stimuli which themselves bring immediate benefit or harm, but also to other physical or chemical agencies – waves of sound, light, and the like – which in themselves only *signal* the approach of these stimuli; though it is not the sight and sound of the beast of prey which is in itself harmful to the smaller animal, but its teeth and claws. (*A*, p. 75.)

Clearly, a signal is of little value if it tells the animal only things that it already knows. Thus, from one point of view, experiments like Rescorla's and Kamin's flesh out Pavlov's basic intuition of the signal function of the CS.

From a more rigorous point of view, however, these experiments show that Pavlov's concept of temporal contiguity is insufficient. We must clearly allow for a rather complex process of analysis in an animal taking part in a conditioning experiment. This process apparently enables the animal to compute the probability that the UCS will follow the CS and compare this with the probability that the UCS will occur anyway; only if the former probability is higher than the latter does the animal bother to take account of the CS. To those familiar with the complexity of the brain, this is not an undue amount of computational ability with which to endow animals; and to those familiar with the achievements of modern computers, it does not necessarily smack of mentalism to do so. But to an earlier generation of behaviourists, these conclusions would have been unwelcome; for they indicate that what was once regarded as a very simple kind of learning, one which could serve as the unit of analysis for more complex kinds, is itself very complex indeed. Yet psychologists are still mindful of Lloyd Morgan's canon, and willing to attribute such advanced computational powers to untutored animals only if they must.

This attitude goes so deep that Wagner and Rescorla (whose experiments did much to establish the case for these powers of computation) have recently developed an elegant mathematical theory of conditioning which preserves the principle of temporal contiguity, and yet predicts most of the phenomena which have seemed to run counter to it. The Rescorla–Wagner theory captures the essential feature of the experimental results described above, and others like them, namely that a CS develops associative strength (as reflected in its power to elicit a CR) only to the extent that it predicts something new about the UCS; but it does so while still having the animal respond to particular events (pairings of CS and UCS at particular points in time) rather than compute statistics on a whole series of events. This is not the place to go into the details of their theory, or the experimental evidence for and against it. It is by no means clear yet that the theory will work; and there is already some evidence that it will not. But it has been sufficiently successful in making new and accurate predictions of experimental results for it to be premature to write off Pavlov's principle of temporal contiguity (in this new guise) completely.

With regard, then, to the conditions which give rise to a CR, Pavlov was right that these turn on the relationship between the CS and UCS; and he may not have been wrong in describing that relationship as one of temporal contiguity. But what is the nature of the association so formed? This is the second of the four questions we distinguished earlier in the chapter. How successfully did Pavlov answer it?

His answer is known as the 'stimulus substitution' theory

of conditioning. This states that, as a result of classical conditioning, the CS comes to elicit the same responses as the UCS. It has been known for years that, stated thus baldly, this view is wrong: if the flash of a light bulb is made regularly to precede the delivery of food to a dog, the dog does *not* usually attempt to eat the light bulb (though it may sometimes go so far as to lick at it). But this may be simply because a light bulb is not, after all, very easy to eat. And a more restricted version of stimulus substitution theory does appear, with rare exceptions, to represent the truth. Roughly speaking, this version is encapsulated in the slogan 'no response to the CS which is not a response also elicited by the UCS' (as distinct from 'all responses elicited by the UCS come to be elicited by the CS'). The exceptions to this modified stimulus substitution rule are mainly concerned with painful UCSs. For some reason, the CRs conditioned with such UCSs are often diametrically opposed to the responses elicited by the UCS itself. The clearest example of this concerns movement: this is radically increased by, say, electric shock, but in response to a CS which signals shock the animal normally freezes, immobile. Apart from the case of painful UCSs (and with some further care in the formulation of the stimulus substitution rule, as we shall see later in the chapter), it is generally true that, after conditioning, the CS elicits some part (but not all) of the responses elicited by the UCS.

The stimulus substitution rule offers a rough guide for predicting the nature of the *response* to the CS. But one can take questions about the nature of the *association* formed during classical conditioning in a deeper sense. One can ask, for example, about the events internal to the animal which become associated.

It was natural for Pavlov to think about such internal events, and equally natural for him to phrase his solution to the problem in terms of hypothetical states in the brain.

But, by and large, once the behaviourist revolution took place, Western psychologists did not find it congenial to ask questions about internal events; and Western physiologists did not consider the science of brain function to be ready to deal with this sort of issue. Recently, however, Western psychology has 'gone cognitive'; not only is it now respectable to ask about internal events, it is *de rigueur*. Thus we find the current generation of American learning theorists wondering about which 'internal representations' participate in the association which underlies an observed CR. Pavlov would not (I think) have liked the language; but he would have approved of the question. His answer, couched in this modern (but old-fashioned) cognitive vocabulary, would be that the association underlying a CR is between the internal representations of the CS and UCS (which, of course, maps directly on to the relationship of temporal contiguity between CS and UCS which he believed to be critical for the formation of the CS). In his own language, as we shall see in the next chapter, this answer claimed that neural activity in the part of the brain ('centre') which receives the CS comes to be redirected to the centre for the UCS.

Historically, the chief alternative view has been that an association is formed directly between (the internal representation of) the CS and the response produced by the UCS. The difference between the two views, anthropomorphically speaking, is that Pavlov held that the CS makes the dog think of food and then salivate, while the alternative position holds that the CS just makes the dog salivate. The popularity of the latter view was greatest when behaviourism in its crudest sense reigned supreme. At that time the preference was for an S–R psychology; that is, one in which each response is directly elicited by a particular stimulus. The complexities of behaviour were then accounted for by supposing that there are long chains of such S–R links, each

R producing a new S, which triggers the next R, and so on. In an analogy popular at the time, the brain was considered to be like a telephone exchange, but one of an extraordinarily rudimentary kind, for it allowed only straight-through connections to be made. Thus it was congenial to treat the association formed during classical conditioning in the same way, i.e. as a direct CS–UCR link.

Given these alternatives, one can take up three positions: that the conditioned association is only CS–UCS, that it is only CS–UCR, or that it is both. The latter view is logically respectable, but it has not been popular, perhaps for the good reason that scientific argument tends to be carried out most productively when opposing theories are stated so as to make clearly different predictions from each other. The extreme behaviourist view, that the association is CS–UCR, is certainly wrong. There are many demonstrations that a conditioned reflex can be established by pairing CS and UCS while preventing, by one means or another, any UCR from occurring; and, if there is no R at the time the S occurs, behaviourist theory has no way of providing for the formation of an S–R link. There are, in contrast, no compelling reasons to reject Pavlov's position, that the association is CS–UCS. It is true that the UCS need not be a stimulus in the usual sense, that is, an event perceived through the sense organs. For it is possible to condition movement of a limb when that movement is provoked by direct electrical stimulation of the brain, this then serving as the UCS. But we do not yet know whether, in such an experiment, electrical stimulation of the brain may produce some kind of perceptual experience, analogous to the perception of a normal UCS, or whether it in some sense directly provokes the observed movement. Pavlov himself, though he did not carry out such experiments, would have regarded the former possibility as plausible. For he treated the 'motor cortex', to which the electrical stimulation is applied in this kind of experiment, as part of the sensory systems, having in particular the task of analysing the sensations which accompany movement. Modern research has, in general supported this view of the functions of the motor cortex.

A phenomenon known as 'sensory preconditioning' throws some light on these issues. In the first stage of the appropriate experiment (see Figure 3) two stimuli of low biological significance (say a tone and a light, each of only moderate intensity) are paired in a standard conditioning

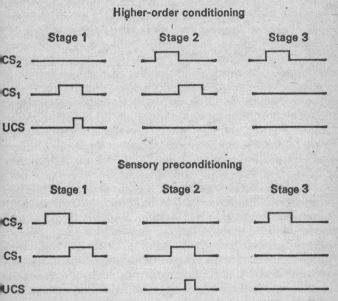

Figure 3. Design of experiments on higher-order conditioning and on sensory preconditioning. In both types of experiment CS_1 is paired with a UCS, CS_2 is paired with CS_1, and evidence of conditioning is provided by the occurrence of CRs to CS_2. The difference between the two procedures lies in the order of Stages 1 and 2.
From Mackintosh (1974).

paradigm so that one (CS_2) regularly precedes the other (CS_1). In the second stage of the experiments CS_1 is paired with a UCS (e.g. an electric shock) and comes to elicit an appropriate CR. Finally, responses to CS_2 are measured. It is often found that CS_2 now also elicits a CR appropriate to the UCS, which has been directly paired, however, only with CS_1. Since CS_2 has never been paired with the responses elicited by the UCS, there has been no possibility of setting up a CS–UCR association. The most plausible interpretation, therefore, of sensory preconditioning is that, because of the CS_2–CS_1 pairings of the first stage of the experiment, CS_2 evokes an internal representation of CS_1; this then (because it has been paired with the UCS) evokes the observed CR.

Notice that this account implies that, in the first stage of the experiment, CS_1 functions as an effective UCS, even though, unlike the UCSs used by Pavlov (food, acid, shock) and by most subsequent workers, it has no biological significance for the animal. This in turn implies that classical conditioning is a quite general process whereby associations are formed between any events that have the right predictive relationships to each other.

Recently, a new approach has been adopted which gives rise to conclusions similar to those derived from sensory preconditioning. One first pairs a CS with a UCS and then does something to alter the significance of the UCS. Finally, one re-tests the response elicited by the CS. The argument behind this type of experiment runs as follows. If the CS elicits an internal representation of ('makes the animal think of') the UCS, and if the UCS now means something different to the animal than at the time of original conditioning, its response to the CS should change correspondingly. But if the association underlying the CR is formed directly between the CS and the responses elicited by the UCS at the time of original conditioning, the changed significance of the UCS should not affect the CR.

Rescorla has recently completed a series of experiments

with rats along these lines. The UCS used was food in some of them, shock or loud noise in others. Between conditioning and testing a number of techniques were used to alter the significance of the UCS. For example, the noise UCS was repeatedly presented to the rats until they ceased to take much notice of it; or the food UCS was offered to them when they had already eaten so much that they had no desire for food. These techniques reduce the effectiveness of the UCS in eliciting its normal UCR. The key question was, would they also reduce the effectiveness of the CS in eliciting its CR? This is indeed what happened, thus supporting the view that a CS elicits an internal representation of the UCS.

Rescorla also carried out experiments of this kind using 'second-order' conditioned stimuli (see Figure 3). Pavlov originally demonstrated that, if conditioning is first carried out with one CS and then a second CS is paired with the first (this now serving as UCS), the second CS acquires the power to elicit the CR, even though it has never been paired directly with the original UCS. This is second-order conditioning. Rescorla set up such a second-order CR in rats, and then used the techniques described above to alter the significance of either the UCS or the first-order CS. His results were quite different from those obtained in the ordinary, first-order, conditioning experiments. The response to the second-order CS was unaffected by changes in the significance of either the UCS or the first-order CS.

Thus it is possible that different rules apply to first- and second-order associations. Whereas first-order associations link representations of the CS and UCS, second-order CSs seem directly to elicit the responses with which, during conditioning to the first-order CS, they have been paired. If this pattern of results stands up under further investigation, we shall be in the surprising situation that simple conditioning fits happily into the framework of cognitions and introspections favoured in 1870 (and again in 1970), while higher-order conditioning fits equally happily into the framework favoured during the high tide of behaviourism. This outcome would be all the more paradoxical because it is higher-order conditioning on which speculative learning theorists have usually relied when they wish to generate the complex symbolic structures of thinking Man.

If we leave aside higher-order conditioning, the picture that we have of what goes on during conditioning is as follows. The animal is sensitive to the contingency (as defined earlier in this chapter) between CS and UCS. If this contingency enables a prediction to be made from occurrences of the CS to a raised probability of occurrence of the UCS, the animal generates in response to the CS an internal representation of the UCS (we might reasonably say that it comes to *expect* the UCS). This by itself does not tell us anything about how the animal will *behave* in response to the CS (there are many ways one might behave in anticipation of a particular event). To help us say something about this we have at our disposal so far only the stimulus substitution rule, according to which the animal will respond to the CS with some subset of the responses which are elicited by the UCS. But, given the demotion of the responses elicited by the UCS as determinants of the association formed during conditioning, we would do well to scrutinize the stimulus substitution rule again.

As so far stated, this rule apparently implies that the CS comes to elicit a set of responses actually elicited by the UCS during the trials on which the CS and UCS are paired. This implication is demonstrably false. The clearest way to make this point is in experiments in which a CS is first paired with shock and then presented to the animal while it makes a response maintained by instrumental reinforcement. In a typical experiment of this kind rats are trained to press a bar for a food reward. The CS is paired with shock while the rat is in a different apparatus, and it is then presented to the animal while it is engaged in barpressing. It is reliably found that the CS disrupts barpressing, a phenomenon described as 'conditioned suppression'.

Clearly, barpressing cannot have been disrupted by the shock, because the animal was not pressing a bar when it was shocked. It could be argued that the disruption of barpressing is due to some other conditioned response (remaining immobile, for example) which is directly transferred from the shock UCS to the CS on conditioning trials, and which is incompatible with barpressing. But this possibility can be ruled out by training the animal to make an instrumental response, not for the reward of food, but in order to avoid shock. Now if we present it with a CS previously paired with shock, far from suppressing the instrumental response, the CS often (though not always) facilitates it. It is difficult to see how any specific response could both suppress and facilitate instrumental behaviour depending on the nature of the reinforcement (food or shock avoidance) for which the behaviour is performed.

If we continue to talk of specific responses conditioned to the CS, results such as these must remain mysterious. If, instead, we simply say that the CS causes the animal to expect shock and to respond *appropriately*, they make perfect sense: if you are working for food and are told to expect an imminent shock, you are likely to lose interest in the work; but if you are working to avoid shock, you are likely to redouble your efforts. The trouble with this, of course, is the vagueness of the word 'appropriately'. What you think is appropriate, and what I think, can differ considerably. It was this kind of vagueness that caused Pavlov to give up consulting his psychologist colleagues in 1900. Nonetheless, it is clear that, couched in terms of specific responses, the stimulus substitution rule must be abandoned.

There is, however, an alternative way of framing the stimulus substitution rule which is able to cope with most of the experimental findings, and which captures at least part of the notion of appropriateness. This is to talk, not in terms of responses, but in terms of the capacity of stimuli to elicit responses. Put in this 'stimulus-property' form, the (modified) stimulus substitution rule reads as follows: any property which a CS comes to possess in consequence of being paired with a UCS is a property also possessed by the UCS itself. This formulation is consistent, for example, with the findings made in the experiments we have just discussed; for if we shock a rat while it is working for food, the work is usually disrupted; but if we shock it while it is working to avoid shock, it usually works harder.

Thus it is possible (still with some troubling exceptions) to preserve the stimulus substitution rule in its stimulus-property form. We lose, however, the power of precise prediction offered by the pristine version of the rule (which states simply that the CS elicits the same responses as the UCS with which it is paired). To re-acquire this predictive power, new theorizing is required, specifying in greater detail the kind of central state that the CS produces, along with its evocation of a representation of the UCS. (The adjective 'central' is a usefully ambiguous one: it refers at once to the inferred mind and the real brain; so a 'central state' is somewhere in the head.) An important move in this direction is to specify certain 'central motivational states' as the responses to CSs which have been paired with certain kinds of biologically important UCSs (food, shock etc.), the observed CRs then flowing from these states. This move has been fiercely resisted by out-and-out behaviourists; but Pavlov (who invariably spoke of central states, meaning, of course, states of the brain) would have been less outraged. The names that have been given to these central motivational states by successive learning theorists are pleasingly homely – 'fear', 'hope', 'frustration' and the like. But, in some cases, these names hide quite elaborate theories which make a reasonably good job of predicting behaviour in a wide variety of circumstances. These theories, however, are beyond the scope of this book.

So far in this chapter we have been concerned exclusively

with the formation of conditioned reflexes. But exactly the same questions come up when we consider their disappearance – the phenomena that Pavlov dealt with under the headings of his various kinds of inhibition. What are the conditions which prevent a CR from occurring? And what is the process which causes this to happen?

As we saw in the previous chapter, Pavlov distinguished two ways in which CRs disappear. The first way, which he attributed to the operation of 'external inhibition', preserves the predictive relationship between CS and UCS but introduces something novel into the experimental situation. The novel element leads to a maximum disruption of the CR the first time it occurs, its effect lessening as the animal becomes familiar with it. Pavlov's explanation of this phenomenon was simple, and it has been universally accepted since: the novel stimulus attracts the animal's attention ('elicits an orienting reflex', as Pavlov put it) and thus interferes with its ability to make the CR. Similar disruptions can be observed in many other forms of behaviour, and there is therefore no reason to regard 'external inhibition' as having anything special to do with conditioned reflexes.

Much more discussion has centred on Pavlov's second class of disappearing CRs, the one he attributed to 'internal inhibition'. This class covers those cases in which the predictive relationship between CS and UCS is or becomes negative, that is (as we shall see below), the probability of the UCS given the CS is lower than the probability of the UCS in the absence of the CS. In keeping with the notion (which we met in Chapter 3) that a CR needs reinforcement from the UCS, Pavlov regarded the critical ingredient for the loss or suppression of a CR as the occurrence of the CS without its being followed by the UCS. But, although he went into considerable detail about the nature of the inhibitory process supposedly produced in the brain under these conditions (see Chapter 5), he was never very explicit about the way in which the absence of the UCS might give rise to inhibition. On the face of it, the absence of the UCS can have no effect of any kind unless it is in some way a disconfirmation of a prior expectation that the UCS will in fact occur. Given our discussion above of the nature of the association that underlies a CR, this way of looking at the non-occurrence of the UCS will be congenial. It is also in agreement with the experimental evidence.

Before considering this evidence, let us ask what license Pavlov had to talk about inhibition at all. After all, the primary observation made when we destroy the positive predictive relationship between CS and UCS (be it in extinction, differentiation or conditioned inhibition) is that the CS ceases to elicit a CR; that is, it gradually comes to do nothing at all. Should we not say, under these circumstances, that the previously formed CR is simply weakened or lost? Or that the animal now expects the UCS less or not at all? Why did Pavlov feel impelled to postulate a whole new process, that of internal inhibition, to account for the facts?

Indeed, it has been strongly urged by some (Skinner is a notable example) that inhibition is an unnecessary construct, and that we should treat extinction etc. as returning the CS to the status it had before conditioning ever began. But there are a number of good reasons not to accept this *status quo ante* view; and a smaller number of good reasons to accept Pavlov's view that the various experimental paradigms he grouped under the rubric of 'internal inhibition' generate a special process which *actively suppresses* the previously acquired CR – this being the heart of his concept of internal inhibition.

Reasons not to accept the *status quo ante* view include the phenomena of spontaneous recovery and disinhibition.

If a CR is extinguished by repeated presentation of the CS without a following UCS, and then the experimenter goes home for the night, he finds on starting up the experiment again next day that there has been recovery of the extinguished CR: this is 'spontaneous recovery'. It was taken by Pavlov as showing that the CR had been temporarily overlaid by a process of inhibition, which then dissipated overnight. The phenomenon is a reliable one, and occurs whenever, during the early stages of extinction, a rather long interval intervenes after a series of extinction trials separated by rather short intervals.

'Disinhibition' is a more surprising observation. For its demonstration we require a novel stimulus (one that would be able to disrupt a CR by external inhibition if it were presented along with a positive CS); and a stimulus which has been subjected to internal inhibition (i.e. one that has been extinguished, differentiated, turned into a conditioned inhibitor, or made the signal for a long-delayed CR). The novel stimulus is presented together with the internal inhibitor (which no longer elicits any conditioned response); and this combination of two agents, each ineffective by itself, elicits a CR. This is the phenomenon of disinhibition. It has never received satisfactory explanation, but it bears a strong resemblance to external inhibition. Like the latter phenomenon, it is maximal when the novel stimulus is first applied and then diminishes with repetition. For this reason Pavlov regarded it as 'external inhibition of internal inhibition', supposing that the (internal) inhibitory process is disrupted when the animal's attention is distracted. This account, however, fails to explain why the novel stimulus does not also disrupt the CR thus released from inhibition, just as it would if the CR were intact in the first place.

Since stimuli which have never been paired with a UCS do not suddenly acquire the capacity to elicit CRs in this way, we may take both spontaneous recovery and disinhibition to indicate that a stimulus which once elicited a CR (but, after extinction, differentiation etc., no longer does so) remains different from a stimulus which never acted as a CS at all. To make the distinction between the two kinds of stimuli, it is common to use the terms 'neutral' (for a stimulus which has never been conditioned to anything)

81

and 'CS—' (for an internal inhibitor, no matter what conditioning history turned it into one).

A CS—, then, is not neutral. But is it an active inhibitor of the CR? The evidence that it is comes from three kinds of experiment: summation tests, retardation tests and reactions of the reverse sign.

A summation test involves taking the CS— and presenting it to the animal together with some positive CS (CS+), i.e. a CS which signals the occurrence of the same UCS whose non-occurrence is signalled by the CS—. If the CS— actively inhibits the CR, it should weaken the response to the CS+. A retardation test involves taking the CS— and attempting to turn it into a CS+ by reinforcing it with the UCS whose absence it previously predicted. If the CS— actively inhibits the CR, it should be particularly difficult to turn it into a CS+ in this way. Both these tests were used by Pavlov and have been used extensively since. The third test of inhibition was not used by Pavlov, but was developed subsequently in both the Soviet Union and the United States. It requires one to show that the CS— elicits a response which is opposite in direction to the response elicited by a CS+ (hence 'reaction of the reverse sign'). In the Soviet Union, for example, Ilina, using human subjects, conditioned a fall in visual sensitivity by pairing a CS+ with a flash of light as UCS; she then found that a CS—, produced by differentiation, elicited a *rise* in visual sensitivity. This kind of finding is rather direct evidence that an internal inhibitor sets up a process which actively opposes the changes elicited by a CS+.

Tests of this kind have in many instances supported Pavlov's view that a CS— is actively inhibitory. But they have not shown that all the procedures that Pavlov regarded as setting up internal inhibition invariably have this effect. The procedure which works best in this respect is that of conditioned inhibition. As we saw in Chapter 3, this procedure intermingles trials of the form, CS+ followed by

UCS, with trials of the form, CS— plus CS+ followed by no UCS. There is also evidence that differentiation (CS+ followed by UCS, intermingled with CS— followed by no UCS) often endows the CS— with inhibitory powers; and that delayed conditioning does this for the early part of the long-acting CS. But the status of extinction remains equivocal: there is no firm evidence that an extinguished CS becomes truly inhibitory, as distinct from merely losing its previous capacity to elicit a CR.

Given that we have tests of inhibition, we can now ask a question which we previously postponed: what are the conditions which give rise to a (true) internal inhibitor? In one sense we have already answered this, in the summary given in the preceding paragraph: an actively inhibitory CS— is produced by the procedures of conditioned inhibition, differentiation and delayed conditioning. But, just as we tried to capture in a formula the essential feature of the relationship between CS and UCS which gives rise to a CR, so we must try to find a formula for the conditions which lead to its inhibition. Such a formula can be found: it is more or less the mirror image of the formula for the formation of CRs.

We have seen that excitatory conditioning (i.e. the process responsible for the establishment of CRs) takes place when the CS+ signals a raised probability of occurrence of the UCS. By a pleasing symmetry, inhibitory conditioning appears to take place when the CS— signals a *lowered* probability of occurrence of the UCS. This is what happens, for example, in conditioned inhibition or in a differentiation. During simple extinction, however, the UCS occurs neither when the erstwhile CS+ is presented nor when it is not. Thus this view of the necessary conditions for the establishment of an internal inhibitor offers an account of the failure of extinguished CSs to pass the tests of active inhibition. It also explains why Pavlov, nonetheless, regarded extinguished CSs as internal inhibitors. For his normal practice was to signal the same UCS by several different CSs in the same experimental session. Thus, when he subjected one of these stimuli to extinction, the extinguished CS did signal (by comparison with the other positive stimuli in the experiment) a lowered probability of occurrence of the UCS.

Firmer evidence in support of this formula for internal inhibition comes from Rescorla's experiments on contingency, which we met earlier in the chapter. Rescorla divided an experimental session into units of time and varied the probability of a shock UCS both in the presence of a CS and in its absence. When the probability of shock was lower in the presence of the CS – $p(UCS/CS) < p(UCS/\overline{CS})$ – the CS acquired the capacity to inhibit conditioned responses. Note that this result was obtained even though shocks occurred at a substantial rate in the presence of the CS. Nonetheless, so long as the shock rate was higher when the CS was absent, this stimulus became an active inhibitor of the CR.

At the start of this chapter four questions were asked. It is convenient to recapitulate the argument of the chapter by summarizing the main features of our answers to them.

1. The necessary condition for a CR to be formed is that the probability of the UCS, given the CS+, should be higher than the probability of the UCS in the absence of the CS+.

2. The association evoked by the CS+ is an internal representation of the UCS; in consequence, the animal responds (in some but not all ways) as it would do if presented with the UCS itself.

3. The most important condition which gives rise to the disappearance of CRs (i.e. to their internal inhibition) is that the probability of the UCS, given the CS−, should be lower than the probability of the UCS in the absence of the CS−.

4. The process which causes the disappearance of CRs

under the conditions described in (3) is actively inhibitory in nature.

In reaching these conclusions we have taken account of many experimental findings not available to Pavlov. Yet there is comparatively little in them that he would find surprising. Comparatively little, that is, apart from the language in which they are couched. His own language referred rather to the brain and its goings on. We look at this language in the next chapter.

5. Pavlov's Theory of Brain Function

At the start of Chapter 4 I drew a distinction between two kinds of theory-building. In the first we seek to reduce the complexities of data to a few underlying principles or rules. This kind of search for unifying principles, as applied to the results of conditioning experiments, occupied our attention in the previous chapter. The second kind of theory attempts to construct a mechanism which might act in conformity with these principles to generate the observed data. Throughout his research on conditioned reflexes Pavlov occupied himself with both kinds of theory-building, usually simultaneously. Thus, although he thought and wrote about the issues which we considered in Chapter 4, the language in which he carried on the argument was very different from the one we used. His own language usually dealt with events which he believed to be going on in the brain. It was very natural for him to think in terms of mechanism, rather than engage simply in the more abstract search for unifying principles. And, since he knew that the actual mechanisms underlying behaviour inhabit the brain, it was equally natural for him to locate the mechanisms which he invented in the same place.

However, when Pavlov started to think about conditioned reflexes, knowledge of the brain was rudimentary. Thus the modern neurophysiologist finds Pavlov's theory of brain function (derived as it was entirely from his research on conditioned reflexes) very strange. So strange, in fact, that this aspect of his theorizing has suffered an almost total neglect, except in the Soviet Union. It will help us to take it more seriously (as it deserves to be taken) if we first draw another distinction between two kinds of theory.

If one knows nothing about the actual processes at work

in producing a set of phenomena, one can construct a 'black-box' model, making no assumptions about the elements of which the system under study is constructed, but from which one can deduce the experimental observations. If this approach is applied to behaviour, the black-box model is *implicitly* a theory of brain function; but it need not be directly concerned with the way the brain or its neurons work. Such a model specifies (if it is successful) the functions that the brain must carry out in order to produce behaviour, but not the way in which it actually discharges these functions. The Canadian psychologist, D. O. Hebb, has called this kind of model a '*conceptual* nervous system'. The alternative to this approach is to construct an *explicit* model of the way in which the *real* nervous system works.

Now Sherrington, in his work on spinal reflexes, constructed a model of the real nervous system. Most psychologists, when they make theories about learning, construct conceptual nervous systems. Pavlov thought he was making a model of the real nervous system, but actually produced a conceptual nervous system. This is not a derogatory remark. A successful conceptual nervous system (that is, one that succeeds in accounting for behavioural observations) marks out the processes which the real nervous system must carry out. It is thus a very large step on the way to understanding how the brain controls behaviour. Given the lack of knowledge in Pavlov's day about even the structure of the brain, it was impossible for him to tackle directly the problem of how the brain produces conditioned reflexes. And even today, when knowledge of the brain is much greater, the most sensible way to approach this kind of problem may well be to construct a conceptual nervous system first, and only then attempt to translate this into an understanding of brain function.

In this chapter, then, we shall consider Pavlov's theory of brain function with two different questions in mind: (1) What are the behavioural observations it seeks to account for, and how well does it do so? (2) How does it stand up if we compare it to our present knowledge of the brain?

The starting point for Pavlov's approach was the concept of the reflex arc (see Chapter 1). The major elements into which a reflex arc may be analysed are: first, a *receptor* organ (e.g. touch receptors in the skin, or the cells composing the retina of the eye), which receives physical energy from the world outside and transmutes it into a nervous message; second, an *afferent* limb which conveys this message to the central nervous system; third, a *transmissive* element which deals with this incoming message and converts it into an outgoing one; fourth, an *efferent* limb which sends instructions to the muscles or glands; and fifth, an *effector* organ composed of these muscles (e.g. the arm) or glands (e.g. those that secrete saliva). In its simplest form, the 'transmissive' element in this chain may consist of a single synapse, that is, a single junction between the afferent and efferent neurons. In the case of the conditioned reflex, the transmissive element is, effectively, the whole brain. In like manner, the simplest form taken by the afferent limb of a reflex arc may consist of a single neuron activated by a single receptor; whereas, when a dog reacts with a conditioned salivary response to the sight of its food-dish, it uses all the complex powers of its visual system to detect and analyse this stimulus. These added complexities caused Pavlov to develop a new vocabulary, congruent with that of the reflex arc but not identical to it, to describe the mechanism which produces conditioned reflexes.

The first of his new terms comes at the start of the reflex arc. Instead of speaking of 'receptors' and 'afferent neurons', he introduced the concept of an 'analyser' (visual, auditory, tactile etc.), thus acknowledging that the stimulus which becomes a CS (or indeed which acts as UCS) is thoroughly analysed by the brain before it is allowed to enter into association with other, equally thoroughly analysed, stimuli. An 'analyser' includes the receptor organ and the afferent neurons which transmit information to the brain, but it also includes those parts of the brain which analyse this information into its component parts, or synthesize it into stable percepts. The visual analyser, for example, is made up of the eye, the fibres which travel in the optic nerve, and all those parts of the brain which transform the nervous impulses carried by these fibres into visual sensations (flashes, colours, steady illumination) or visual objects (the sight of a table, a tree, a person etc.).

Today we know that many levels of the brain participate in this kind of perceptual elaboration, the highest level being located in the cerebral cortex. Pavlov also knew of the importance of the cerebral cortex for perceptual functions; indeed, he over-emphasized its role, allocating to the rest of the brain far less than we now know to be its due share in the control of complex behaviour. This tendency was common to many scientists at the time, and persisted well into the twentieth century.

Both the CS and the UCS, then, first act on their relevant analysers. In consequence, in Pavlov's view, they set up neural activity in the cortical portions of the analysers. Pavlov spoke of the cortical points at which this activity – or 'excitation' – was set up as the 'centres' for the CS and UCS. As we shall see, 'the excitatory process' set up in this way by conditioned or unconditioned stimuli provides one of the two fundamental poles of Pavlovian theory, the other being the 'inhibitory process'. It is by attributing various properties to these two forms of nervous activity that Pavlov attempted to account for the varied phenomena that he observed in his conditioning experiments.

The most basic observation that any theory of conditioning has to explain is that the CS comes to elicit a response which it did not originally elicit, but which *is* normally elicited by the UCS. It is common ground that this requires one to postulate the formation of a new connection in the nervous system (one that was not there, or at least not active, before conditioning). This new connection in some way enables the CS to produce a new response, the CR Pavlov recognized this implication of his experiments, and proposed a mechanism for the creation of the new connection. He proposed, first, that the strength of the excitation set up by the UCS is greater than that set up by the CS; and, second, that 'every strongly excited centre in some manner attracts towards itself every other weaker excitation reaching the system simultaneously.' (*G* II, p. 47.) In consequence, the excitation reaching the CS centre is drawn to the UCS centre, so forming the new connection and giving rise to the CR. Pavlov's proposal is in good agreement with the conclusion reached in the previous chapter that the CS evokes a central representation of the UCS. However, it is in less good agreement with the experimental data in assuming that the excitation set up by a UCS is always stronger than that set up by a CS. For, as we also saw in the last chapter, it is possible in a sensory preconditioning experiment to produce a conditioned reflex by pairing stimuli of apparently equal biological strength (e.g. a tone and a light).

This, then, is how Pavlov thought that the afferent limb of his *conditioned* reflex arc (up to the cortical centre for the CS) makes contact with its efferent limb (from the UCS centre to the salivary glands). But we can already see in his proposal that feature of his theorizing which was to estrange it from modern neurophysiology : namely, the tendency to treat the nervous process as independent of the physical arrangement of the nerve-cells in which this process occurs. Sherrington's concept of the synapse, dating from 1897, was firmly *morphological* – it referred to the point at which two neurons come into physical as well as functional contact. But Pavlov's statement that excitation in the UCS centre 'attracts to itself' the excitation in the CS centre ignores the question of how this action at a distance can take place. Nor, subsequently, did he pay any attention to this problem. Yet it had already become clear in the first decade of this century that the brain consists of a multitude of individual cells, connected to each other in a bewildering variety of patterns but nonetheless providing a set of distinct pathways along which the nervous message must proceed, not a homogeneous medium in which it can proceed in all directions at once. This 'connectionist' approach to the workings of the brain is fundamental to the concept of the reflex arc, especially as worked out by Pavlov's contemporary, Sherrington. The great paradox of Pavlov's work is that his avowed intention was to bring the reflex arc into the brain; and yet, right at the start of this attempt, he abandoned the major postulate of reflex theory, namely, that reflex action derives from the spatial arrangement of nerve cells and their interconnections.

This aspect of Pavlov's thought is nowhere clearer than in his treatment of inhibition, especially internal inhibition. Pavlov struggled with this 'cursed problem', as he called it, for a good thirty years, and he had not solved it when he died. His views changed many times over that period, often back to positions held earlier and abandoned. It is not possible to trace all these changes here. I shall try, rather, to bring out only the main features of his approach. Perhaps the best way to do this is to contrast his concept of inhibition with the one held by neurophysiologists today.

Today we suppose excitation of a neuron to mean the passage of a series of electrochemical impulses from the body of the nerve-cell along its axon. These impulses arrive at the synaptic junction with the next cell. There, they cause the release of a small chemical packet, known as a neuro-transmitter, into the space between the two cells. The neuro-transmitter excites the next ('post-synaptic') cell, thus starting the same process up again. In this way a whole chain of neurons can pass the nervous message along. 'Inhibition' then refers to processes which interfere with the passage of the nervous message from one cell to the next. This can happen in essentially two ways. The release of neuro-transmitter can be prevented by a change in the transmitting ('pre-synaptic') neuron; or the neuro-transmitter can be robbed of its effect by a change in the post-synaptic neuron. Either way, pre-synaptic or post-synaptic inhibition, as it is understood today, consists in a *blockade* of the passage of a neural message.

Pavlov's internal inhibition is quite different. It is not simply an interruption in the passage of neural excitation. It is a nervous process in its own right, opposite in sign to the excitatory process but equal in status. Just as excitation can be passed from one part of the nervous system to another, so can Pavlovian inhibition. Moreover, its journey through the nervous system goes via the same neurons that transmit excitation. Thus these neurons are capable of operating in two radically different states: in one they transmit excitation, in the other inhibition.

Let us apply these two views of inhibition to a typical Pavlovian experiment. Suppose we have a conditioned inhibitor (CS−) which, when presented together with a CS+, prevents this from eliciting a CR. We accept that part of Pavlov's theory which claims that the CS+ causes the passage of a neural message from its cortical centre to the UCS centre. The modern view of inhibition would lead us to expect, therefore, that the CS− will in some way interfere with this message. For this to occur, the CS− must set in train its own nervous message, which will itself pass along a chain of neurons (and is therefore *excitatory* in character) until it makes contact with the chain carrying the message from the CS+ to the UCS centre. There, by setting up either pre- or post-synaptic inhibition, it will block the further passage of this message. Pavlov's view of what goes on in this kind of experiment was not like this at all. He supposed that the CS− sets up an inhibitory process *in the cortical centre for the CS− itself*. From there inhibition flows out to other points of the cortex, reaching among other places the centre for the CS+. Once this happens, the CS+ centre is temporarily altered, so that its cells react to incoming stimulation (i.e. to the CS+), not with excitation, but with inhibition. Thus the CR fails to appear, not because the chain from the CS+ to the UCS centre is broken, but because the mode of reaction of the CS+ centre is itself changed. (In psychological terms, this means, I suppose, that the CS+ looks or feels different if it is accompanied by a conditioned inhibitor.)

When Pavlov considered the formation of conditioned reflexes, his discussion usually preserved some contact with the anatomical basis of nervous conduction. But in his discussions of internal inhibition this basis virtually disappears from view. The inhibitory process is treated as a wave-like activity propagating spherically from its point of origin (the cortical centre for a CS−) through a homogeneous medium.

Consider as an example his account of experiments performed in his laboratory by Ivanov-Smolensky in 1924. These were concerned with the generalization of inhibition. We saw in Chapter 3 that, if a CR is established to a CS+ and then other stimuli, more or less similar to the CS+ are tested, these elicit a CR whose magnitude is roughly proportional to their degree of similarity to the original CS+. This is the phenomenon of generalization of excitation. Generalization of inhibition is its mirror image. One first establishes an internal inhibitor (CS−) and then tests the inhibitory effect of other stimuli which are more or less similar to the CS−; and one finds that, the greater the similarity of the stimulus to the CS−, the greater is the inhibition that it produces. In Ivanov-Smolensky's experiments salivary CRs were first established to six stimuli: four tones, of frequencies 123, 132, 1036 and 1161 cycles per second, a hissing sound and the tick of a metronome. Then, from time to time, one of these stimuli was extinguished and its effect on the other stimuli was investigated. Suppose, for example, that the tone of 123 c.p.s. was extinguished and now served, therefore, as a CS−. This tone would now be presented to the animal, followed at various times by each of the other five stimuli (all still serving as CS+s). The amount of saliva elicited by each stimulus was measured in the usual way. The results showed that there was an 'inhibitory after-effect' of presentation of the CS— : that is to say, the response to the various CS+s was diminished for a period of time after presentation of the CS—. What is more, the degree to which the CR was reduced in this way depended both on the exact interval elapsing between presentation of the CS— and CS+, and on the degree of similarity between the CS— and CS+.

Some of Ivanov-Smolensky's findings are shown in Figure 4. This shows four important features of his results. First, the inhibitory after-effect was greater, the more similar the CS+ and CS—. Second, the after-effect reached a maximum at about five minutes after presentation of the CS— and then declined. Third, the after-effect became noticeable sooner, the more similar the CS+ and CS— Fourth, the duration of the inhibitory after-effect was greater, the more similar the CS+ and CS—.

In his interpretation of these results Pavlov imagined that the representation of auditory stimuli in the auditory analyser (i.e. the part of the cerebral cortex concerned with the analysis of sounds) is organized in such a way that perceptual similarity corresponds to spatial proximity. The CS— is supposed to set up an inhibitory process in its cortical centre, in the manner that we have seen. This inhibitory process then spreads out like a wave or a sheet unrolling over the surface of the cortex equally in all directions from its point of origin (Pavlov called this 'irradiation of inhibition'). Points closer to the CS— centre (i.e. points which receive stimuli relatively similar to the CS—) are covered by this inhibitory sheet sooner; points further away from the CS— centre are covered later. As the sheet unrolls, the inhibitory effect gets smaller, so the degree of loss of response is less to stimuli whose similarity to the CS— is less. After the sheet has unrolled to its maximum extent, it rolls itself up again towards the CS— centre from which it came (Pavlov called this 'concentration of

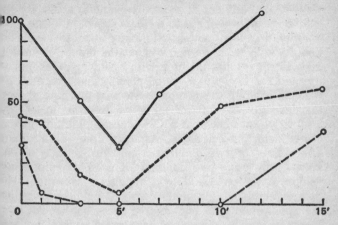

Figure 4. The dependence of the intensity of inhibitory after-effect upon the time elapsed between the application of the negative and the positive conditioned stimulus and upon the similarity of these stimuli (according to Ivanov-Smolensky's experiments). Abscissa: time (in minutes) elapsed since the last application of the conditioned stimulus submitted to experimental extinction (musical tone of 123 vibrations). Ordinate: the size of the conditioned response to stimuli subjected to the inhibitory after-effect, in percentages of their normal response. – – – – musical tone of 132 vibrations (the nearest to inhibitory stimulus). ------ musical tone of 1161 vibrations (more remote from inhibitory stimulus). —— hissing sound.
From Konorski (1948).

inhibition'). It stays longest at points close to the CS–; hence the duration of the inhibitory after-effect is correspondingly longer for stimuli which are more similar to the CS–.

There can be little doubt of the importance of Ivanov-Smolensky's observations, and similar results have been obtained in other experiments using different kinds of stimuli. What is more, Pavlov's explanation offers in many ways a good account of these observations, as the reader can verify by applying it to the data shown in Figure 4. It is a pity, therefore, that almost nothing about this explanation fits with what we know about the brain. No known nervous activity has the properties Pavlov gives his inhibitory process. In any case, simple conditioning experiments, without entering the nervous system at all, have shown that his theory of internal inhibition is wrong in its first assumption, namely, that a CS— causes inhibition in the centre which receives it. Asratyan, one of Pavlov's students, set up two different conditioned reflexes to the same CS by using two different UCSs (shock, producing flexion of the paw; and food, producing salivation). He then extinguished one of the two CRs only, by omitting the appropriate UCS but not the other one. If Pavlov's theory were right, this should have set up inhibition in the cortical centre for the CS. From this it follows that *both* CRs should be inhibited (since they share a common CS). But Asratyan showed that this was not the case: the extinguished CR disappeared, while the other CR was unaffected.

We are thus in the unsatisfactory position of having a number of established facts which seem to provide significant clues to the underlying processes which produce them, but no theory which accounts for them adequately. For all its faults, Pavlov's theory is still the best we have. Modern theories of association have largely ignored the temporal parameters which are so critical in experiments like Ivanov-Smolensky's. And they have added nothing to the basic notion of generalization introduced by Pavlov: that we respond (or inhibit responding) similarly to similar stimuli. As to theories of brain function, they still have a long way to go before they can deal with events of the complexity illustrated in Figure 4.

If Pavlov's theory is the best we have, it is worth exploring it further. Like many scientists, Pavlov liked his theories to be symmetrical. Having discovered that the inhibitory process irradiates and then concentrates, he supposed this to be true also of excitation. To show that this was so two of his colleagues, Petrova and Podkopayev, carried out experiments on the 'excitatory after-effect'.

This phenomenon is the mirror-image of the inhibitory after-effect studied by Ivanov-Smolensky. To demonstrate it one requires a number of CS−s and one CS+. Each of the CS−s is presented at various times after the CS+. It is found that the response to the CS− is increased (i.e. there is disinhibition) to a degree which depends on the time elapsing after the presentation of the CS+, and on the similarity between the CS− and CS+. For example, Petrova arranged five apparatuses for tactile stimulation of the hind leg of a dog, from the paw to the pelvis. Stimulation of the paw served as CS+, acid in the mouth as UCS. Stimulation of the other four points served as CS−s (by differentiation) and normally elicited no salivation whatsoever. However, if Petrova first stimulated the paw (CS+) and then, 15–60 seconds later, one of these inhibitory points, there was now a salivary response. This response was larger, and the period during which it occurred was longer, the closer the inhibitory point to the paw.

Pavlov interpreted these findings, and others like them, as indicating that excitation irradiates out from the cortical centre for the CS+ and temporarily 'washes away' the inhibitory process located in the centres for the various CS−s. The closer the inhibitory point to the paw, the closer is the corresponding point on the cortex to the centre for the CS+. The irradiating wave of excitation reaches close points sooner, produces a larger effect, and stays there longer, than at distant points. Eventually, the excitatory wave reverses its flow and concentrates again in the centre for the CS+. Thus the excitatory after-effect, like the inhibitory one, is only short-lived.

Another phenomenon which Pavlov attempted to explain in terms of irradiation and concentration of excitation is that of generalization. During the early stages of conditioning it is possible to replace the CS with a wide variety of other stimuli, and these too prove to be capable of eliciting the CR. As pairings of the CS with the UCS are repeated, however, the range of generalization of the CS becomes more restricted, until only rather similar stimuli are able to elicit the CR. Pavlov interpreted these findings as indicating that, in the early stages of conditioning, the excitatory process set up by the CS irradiates widely over the cerebral cortex; as conditioning proceeds, however, excitation becomes more concentrated in the centre for the CS+. The trouble with this account is that generalization is independent of the interval between presentations of the training CS and the test stimulus. Since the excitatory after-effect described in the preceding paragraph is rather strictly dependent on the interval between presentation of the CS+ and the CS−, it is difficult to see how both phenomena could be due to the same underlying process.

Pavlov believed, then, that the excitatory and inhibitory processes both irradiate from their initiating points in the cortex and then return to base. Should they meet each other *en route* there is a sort of battle between them: if excitation overcomes inhibition, we have the excitatory after-effect; if inhibition is the victor, we see the inhibitory after-effect. But the relations between the two processes are not always antagonistic. Sometimes they reinforce each other in a co-operative process that Pavlov, using Sherrington's term, called 'induction'. Like the two after-effects, induction comes in two varieties.

'Positive induction' is seen under almost the same experimental conditions as the inhibitory after-effect. An internal inhibitor is presented and, shortly after it, the response to a CS+ is tested. Only now it is found that the response to the CS+ is *increased* – sometimes two-fold – above its normal level. The conditions giving rise to this phenomenon and to the inhibitory after-effect, respectively, seem to differ principally in the interval separating the CS− from the CS+. Positive induction occurs sooner than the inhibitory after-effect. Pavlov gives values of several seconds to one or two minutes after the CS— for positive induction; whereas Figure 4 shows that, in Ivanov-Smolensky's experiment, the maximum inhibitory after-effect occurred at five minutes after the CS—. This implies that, if we accept the Pavlovian vocabulary, positive induction occurs while the inhibitory process set up by the CS— is still 'concentrated' in its point of origin in the cortex. From this, Pavlov deduced that a concentrated inhibitory process induces a state of latent excitation in the tissue surrounding it; the excitatory process set up by the CS+, if it is presented at such a time, summates with this latent excitation and causes a super-normal response. This is positive induction.

Again searching for symmetry, Pavlov supposed that, if inhibition can induce excitation around itself, so excitation should induce inhibition. He named this process 'negative induction', and interpreted a variety of different findings as indicating its reality. In one of the relevant experiments, the attempt is made to turn an erstwhile CS— into a CS+ by reinforcing it with the UCS. Two conditions are compared. In one of them presentations of the old CS— are interspersed with presentations of a different CS+; in the other, only the old CS— is repeatedly paired with the UCS. It is found that the former condition greatly retards positive conditioning to the old CS— as compared to the latter. Pavlov's interpretation of this result is that the interspersed presentations of the CS+ give rise to a concentrated excitatory process which induces a zone of inhibition in the surrounding cortex. The centre for the CS— is assumed to lie within this zone. As a result, the inhibitory effect of the CS— is intensified, making positive conditioning harder to achieve.

These inductive relationships are among the most intriguing observations made in Pavlov's laboratory. Using quite different procedures, and working with rats running in alleys or pigeons pecking at keys, psychologists have recently discovered a number of phenomena (generally known as 'contrast effects') which bear important resemblances to both kinds of Pavlovian induction. Thus it seems likely that these tap, as Pavlov thought they did, some quite fundamental feature of the activity of the central nervous system. It is less likely, however, that Pavlov's theory of the processes underlying induction is correct. But this part of his general theory of brain function is easier for contemporary neurophysiologists to accept than some of his other ideas. For it is similar to the neurophysiological concept of 'lateral inhibition'. It is lateral inhibition, for example, which helps produce good visual contrast between a bright point of light and a poorly illuminated background: cells in the retina surrounding those stimulated by the bright light are inhibited (via their connections with the stimulated cells) from responding to the smaller amount of light which falls on them. Much the same kind of process has also been found to occur in the visual cortex. The resemblance to negative induction will be obvious. Unlike negative induction, however, lateral inhibition has been properly related to the interconnections between cells in a way that Pavlov did not attempt. Thus it remains to be seen whether similar processes underlie inductive phenomena in conditioning experiments.

It will not have escaped the reader that, by this time, Pavlov's theory was getting dangerously flexible. The excitatory and inhibitory processes irradiate and concentrate; they may interfere with each other or reinforce each other; they may produce after-effects or inductive effects, in complex dependence on space and time. Nor did the complications stop there. At various times Pavlov attempted to extend his theory of internal inhibition to cover external inhibition as well; and, though he eventually came round again to treating the two forms of inhibition as separate, the theory underwent severe distortion in the process. To increase the confusion, he added a third kind of inhibition to his classification, 'transmarginal inhibition', about which we shall have more to say in the next chapter. As new experiments were performed, the increasing number of facts proved too complex even for this web of concepts to bind. In an almost desperate attempt to contain them, Pavlov enunciated the 'law of irradiation and concentration of excitation', according to which a weak excitatory process irradiates, a strong one concentrates, and a very strong one irradiates again; and (symmetry once more) there was a parallel law supposedly governing the irradiation and concentration of inhibition. This is not the place to go into the facts that these 'laws' were intended to explain. Nor would it be profitable to do so. For it is the view of most authorities that, at this point, Pavlov overstepped the boundary between a testable theory that makes precise predictions and a catch-all that can explain anything, so long as it does so after the event. And that boundary marks the divide between science and dogma.

Pavlov's theory of brain function must, then, be accounted a failure; but the failure was not total. The first function of a theory is to guide the systematic search for new observations. Pavlov's theory fulfilled this function to the highest degree. His ideas about excitatory and inhibitory processes spreading across the cerebral tissue and mutually interacting led him to investigate the effects of stimulus similarity, the juxtaposition of excitatory and inhibitory stimuli in time and space, the interval separating different kinds of stimulation and so on. In this way he was able to demonstrate phenomena such as stimulus generalization, generalization of inhibition, the excitatory and inhibitory after-effects, positive and negative induction, and other effects that we have not had space to describe. Many of these phenomena have since been replicated in other laboratories; and many of the same principles have been found to operate in situations bearing little apparent resemblance to Pavlov's conditioning paradigms. Furthermore, as we shall see in the next chapter, by taking the Pavlovian theory of conditioning seriously and using it to understand and predict differences between individual animals (and even individual human beings), it has been possible to develop a powerful theoretical and experimental approach to the study of personality.

But the second function of a theory is to explain the observed phenomena. From this point of view Pavlov's theory has been less successful. If one takes a particular set of phenomena – the facts, say, that he treated in terms of positive induction – the theory does not fare badly. But, as Konorski pointed out in his excellent critique, *Conditioned Reflexes and Neuron Organization* (1948), when one juxtaposes Pavlov's treatment of one kind of observation with his treatment of others, irresolvable contradictions emerge. Pavlov was aware of some of these contradictions, and of the danger of glossing over them by attending at any one time to only a restricted set of facts; and he constantly strove to test his 'laws' by bringing them into critical alignment with new data. But some of his successors in the Soviet Union have been less critical in their treatment of his heritage. As Konorski put it, 'whereas in Pavlov's hands the above-mentioned laws were nonetheless living and rich in content, and he continually attempted to find certain general principles governing the application of those laws, some of his pupils juggle arbitrarily with these concepts and quite mechanically stick corresponding labels on various categories of phenomena.'

It has been well said that a theory is never killed off by the facts or its own deficiencies, but only by a better theory. We do not yet have a better theory of conditioning than Pavlov's. There have been various attempts to formulate such a theory, but none has gained wide acceptance over more than a limited range of data. And only Konorski has tried, like Pavlov, to produce a theory of conditioning that is also a theory of the brain.

Unfortunately, as we have seen, the brain in Pavlov's theory is not the brain we know today, it is more a kind of soup. It is not surprising that Pavlov started off thinking of the brain in this way. For, in 1900, there was still sufficient doubt about many key issues in neural anatomy and function for one plausibly to imagine waves of excitation or inhibition propagating through the brain. Many anatomists believed that nerve-cells were joined in a kind of three-dimensional netting along which the nervous message *could* conceivably flow roughly spherically. The nature of the nervous message itself was unknown, as were the events at the synaptic junction, if one accepted that such a junction existed. Thus Pavlov's waves might easily flow out and back across the same physical space. What is more surprising is that Pavlov continued to state his theories in such terms. For, in the first decade of the twentieth century, anatomical and physiological investigation made great progress in unravelling the reflex arc. Cajal's observations established the separateness of nerve-cells; and Sherrington's experiments showed how one can analyse spinal reflex action in terms of events in specific nerve-cells and their synaptic connections. Pavlov knew of this work; and, indeed, he makes approving reference to Sherrington's pioneering experiments. But it is as though, in 1900 or thereabouts, he stopped listening to what was going on elsewhere. After all, his own experiments were enough to keep him busy.

6. Personality and Psychopathology

It would be enough to qualify Pavlov as a 'modern master' that he founded the study of conditioned reflexes. But he also originated two other important branches of behavioural science : the study of the biological basis of personality, and the experimental study of neurosis. Although this part of Pavlov's research was intimately bound up with his work on conditioned reflexes, it is much less widely known. To the layman the reflex response to the name 'Pavlov' is 'conditioned reflex'; it is to 'Freud' that he replies 'neurosis'. Yet it is Pavlov, not Freud, who will be of lasting importance for the scientific study of both personality and neurosis.

Just as Pavlov's work on conditioned reflexes was a natural outgrowth of his experiments on the digestive system, so his work on personality and neurosis grew out of his experiments on conditioning. Once again, it was his *method* of research that gave rise to these developments.

Most experimental psychologists working with animals use large groups, usually of rats or mice; they study them for a short time in restricted tasks, they use homogeneous samples of animals (often inbred to be as little different from one another as possible), and they work up the results of their experiments by making statistical comparisons between the average scores of the different groups. It is not surprising that, under these conditions, they fail to notice differences between *individual* animals. In consequence, the study of personality or 'individual differences' is barely represented in the animal laboratories of North American or British departments of psychology. Thus there has come about an unfortunate division between research on individual differences (almost exclusively carried out with human subjects) and those parts of psychology concerned with the biological bases of behaviour (for which research with animals is almost indispensable): a division which allows the ideas of Freud and other such strange growths to flourish profusely on the personality side of the fence.

Pavlov's method was quite different from this standard 'Western' model of animal research. To begin with, he used dogs, not rats, and mongrel dogs at that, which had reached maturity outside the laboratory, so that one animal was different from another in almost every imaginable respect. Second, he worked with his animals for a very long time – several years was not uncommon – so that he and his colleagues came to know the personality of each dog very well. It is for this reason that the subjects of his experiments were known, not by number, as is the usual fashion, but by name. Often the name alone says much about the dog's individuality: 'Gunshot', a 'lively' beast; or 'Milord', a 'calm, inactive' one. Third, each dog was studied in a variety of different tasks, so that consistencies in the behaviour of an individual animal could come to light under experimentally controlled conditions. Finally, the basic data in Pavlov's conditioning experiments came from individual animals – there was no averaging of the results of a group. All the fundamental phenomena of conditioning we met in previous chapters were established in this way. The reliability of a phenomenon was demonstrated by showing that what had been observed in one animal also happened in another treated in the same way. And, usually, this turned out to be true: the *general* laws of the formation of conditioned reflexes, their inhibition and so on, described earlier in this book, *do* hold across all dogs (and all rats, mice and men). But this method of working inevitably also brought to Pavlov's attention the ways in which one dog was different from another. Faced with such differences between individuals (and some of them were profound), there are two common reactions. One is to declare the problem not amenable to scientific investigation, and turn to something else. The other is to treat differences between subjects as 'noise' masking the underlying regularities of nature and ignore them; the technological way of doing this is to use large groups and statistics. Pavlov reacted in neither of these ways. Just as he had decided that 'psychic secretion' could not be pushed under the carpet, but needed systematic investigation, so he concluded that, if his dogs differed from one another, he must find out how and why.

As to the 'how', this was a matter for experiments, and we shall see in a moment what they showed. As to the 'why', Pavlov's answer to this question flowed naturally from his previous research and his existing theory of conditioned reflexes. Since, in its general form, the answer he gave has influenced all subsequent theorists concerned with the biological basis of personality, it is worth looking at it closely.

As we saw in the previous chapter, to account for the phenomena of conditioning Pavlov postulated a number of things going on in the brain (or at least in the head, if we treat his theory as only a conceptual nervous system), things like the 'excitatory process', the 'internal inhibitory process', 'external inhibition' and the like. Now, it is clear that these processes must exist in every dog's brain, since all dogs form conditioned reflexes, develop internal inhibition etc.; indeed, they must exist in essentially the same form in the brains of all higher animals, since the basic laws of conditioning are the same in all species. So we cannot account for Milord's inactivity by saying that he lacks an excitatory process. But what we can do – and what Pavlov did – is to suppose that these basic processes vary from animal to animal in the exact parameters of their functioning. Thus, one dog may have an excitatory process which is particularly easily set into motion, or particularly intense, or particularly rapid in its irradiation; another may have an inhibitory process which is particularly difficult to set into motion, or particularly weak; and so on. In this way, while preserving a unified theory of conditioning, one can nonetheless attempt to account for the peculiarities of the behaviour of individuals.

There is nothing surprising about this move. It is what we all do when we say that such a one is 'quick to anger' or such another 'hard to frighten' : anger and fear are common to us all, but we vary in our readiness to display them. It is also what was done by Pavlov's ancient and illustrious predecessor, Hippocrates (whom Pavlov was fond of acknowledging), in his famous theory of the four temperaments (sanguine, phlegmatic, melancholic and choleric), thought to be due to the accumulation of the different 'humours', blood, phlegm, black and yellow bile. But it was Pavlov who legitimized this move for modern science and pinned it firmly to the nervous system. And virtually all contemporary approaches to the biological basis of personality can trace their origin either directly to his theory, or to the model for theory-building that this provided.

Pavlov's interest in the individual characteristics of his animals dates from the first years of his work on conditioned reflexes. Initially, it was not very different from the interest that a keen dog-lover might take. The descriptions of an animal's personality were based on observations of its general behaviour (rather than on its performance in a conditioning experiment); and dogs were said to be 'lively', or 'calm', 'a ridiculous coward' and so on. Pavlov never abandoned this homely way of talking about his dogs. But, from about 1910, a more systematic approach began to make itself felt. Descriptions of personality were now more often based on observations made in the conditioning experiments; various different hypotheses were tried out to explain the individual characteristics of a particular dog; and various different schemes were used to classify all dogs into different 'types' or 'temperaments'. Not surprisingly (for this was more treacherous and unknown territory than even the conditioned reflex) these hypotheses and classificatory schemes underwent continual modification and tergiversation, never arbitrarily, but always in the light of the latest data and developments in Pavlov's general theory of conditioning. Nor was the interaction between individual differences and the basic laws of conditioning entirely one-way: Pavlov often modified his views about the latter in the light of his developing knowledge of the former. Pavlov's great Soviet successor in this field, B. M. Teplov, has traced these developments in considerable detail. Here we can only consider the form his theory of personality had attained at the time of his death; although, no more than his theory of conditioning at that time, can this be considered a 'final' form, for it was still changing year by year.

By this time Pavlov had reached the view that variation in three 'properties' of the nervous system could account for the individual differences seen in his conditioning experiments. These were the 'strength of the excitatory process'; the 'balance' or 'equilibrium' between the excitatory and (internal) inhibitory processes; and the 'mobility' of these two nervous processes. The first two of these concepts have had distinguished careers in the subsequent development of theories of human personality; the third has so far had less influence.

The fundamental idea behind the notion of 'strength of the excitatory process' (or 'strength of the nervous system', a more usual, though less precise, synonym) is that the cortical cells which are excited by environmental stimuli have a limit to their capacity to withstand excitation. Like the whole animal, they can be over-stimulated, become fatigued, and stop functioning. Pavlov conceived this idea quite early on in his work on conditioned reflexes, but it was some time before it was tied down to particular experimental paradigms and integrated into his general theory of brain function. By 1930 (and there were a number of very different proposals before that time), Pavlov had settled on the dog's reaction to a very strong conditioned stimulus as the critical experimental observation. The notion now was, roughly, that a very strong stimulus gives rise to a very intense excitatory process; in an animal with a low limit to the capacity of the cortical cells to withstand excitation, such a stimulus would be *too* strong and consequently cause a disturbance in behaviour. Such an animal was said to have 'a weak nervous system'.

More precisely, Pavlov tied this concept into the 'law of strength', i.e. the fact that, normally, the more intense the CS, the greater is the CR (see Chapter 3). Pavlov supposed that the intensity of the excitatory process set up by a CS in the cortex is directly proportional to the physical intensity of the CS; and, further, that under normal circumstances the magnitude of the CR is directly proportional to the intensity of the excitatory process. These assumptions, of course, lead directly to the law of strength. But when very intense stimuli are used as CSs, and *in some animals only*, the law of strength breaks down. That is to say, in these animals, very intense stimuli produce CRs which are not greater than those produced by less intense stimuli, and may even be smaller.

To account for this breakdown in the law of strength Pavlov introduced yet another inhibitory process, known as 'transmarginal inhibition'. He supposed that nerve cells cannot increase their level of functioning indefinitely without the danger of physical damage. When the danger point is reached, the process of excitation is therefore replaced by an inhibitory process which protects the cells from harm. This is transmarginal or 'protective' inhibition. In his final classification of inhibitory processes Pavlov grouped transmarginal together with external inhibition, but only on procedural grounds (like external inhibition, it does not involve any change in the basic CS–UCS predictive relationship). As to underlying process, he remained in the same doubt about how transmarginal inhibition relates to external or internal inhibition as he did about the relationship between the latter two forms of inhibition themselves.

A dog with a weak nervous system, then, was now

thought of as one which has a low 'working capacity' in its cortical cells and which in consequence easily generates transmarginal inhibition, as shown by a fall in CR magnitude at high CS intensities. Using this concept, workers in Pavlov's laboratory spoke of dogs as *either* 'weak' *or* 'strong'. This gives the impression that animals come in discrete 'types'; and Pavlov himself wrote of different 'types of nervous system' in just this way. However, Teplov has made a careful analysis of Pavlov's actual reasoning about individual differences and has demonstrated that his theory of personality is not truly dichotomous in this manner; rather, it postulates a number of underlying *dimensions* (to use H. J. Eysenck's term) along which individuals may vary continuously. In the case of strength of the nervous system, for example, it is in principle possible to allocate to each individual a number describing the CS intensity at which the law of strength breaks down; there is no need to suppose that dogs are divided into those in which transmarginal inhibition appears at some very low value of stimulus intensity, and those in which it never appears at all. In practice, it is difficult to do the experiments with this degree of precision, and it becomes more convenient to talk just of 'strong' or 'weak' animals, meaning those at the extremes of the dimension of strength of the nervous system.

There is no point in thinking of an underlying dimension of variation in this way, if it determines performance in only one task. If the breakdown in the law of strength were all we had to go on in determining the strength of the nervous system, we might just as well talk straightforwardly about a breakdown in the law of strength. The notion of strength of the nervous system (or any other such concept) is of value only if there are consistent patterns of individual differences which stretch across *many* tasks: that is, if one can predict from the differences observed between individuals in one situation the differences which will be observed in other situations not yet tried out. It is necessary, therefore, to have other methods of determining the strength of the nervous system, besides the breakdown in the law of strength. A number of such methods were tried out at one time or other in Pavlov's laboratory. Their interrelations were by no means clear at the time of his death. But many of them have been taken up since and developed further, in experiments using both dogs and human subjects. Two of Pavlov's ideas in particular have received substantial confirmation since his death.

The first is that it is possible to build up an intense excitatory process (and thus give rise to transmarginal inhibition), not only by using an intense CS, but also by repeatedly presenting a CS which is itself of only moderate intensity. The argument here is that the excitatory process generated each time a CS is presented does not dissipate immediately. Thus, if a second presentation of the CS occurs very shortly after, the residual excitation from the first CS presentation may summate with the new excitation set up by the second. If this is now repeated over a number of CS presentations (each separated from the former by a short interval), the excitatory process may get bigger and bigger until it passes the threshold of transmarginal inhibition. If that occurs, we should expect to see a fall in the magnitude of the CR. Just this is observed, and, again, in some dogs but not all. Teplov's work with human subjects has greatly extended this method of studying the strength of the nervous system.

The other method developed in Pavlov's laboratory to determine strength of the nervous system makes use of caffeine. This drug was thought by Pavlov to intensify the excitatory process set up by any particular stimulus. It follows that if, in a given animal, a particular CS intensity is just below the threshold of transmarginal inhibition, giving caffeine might take it over the threshold. Again, therefore, we should observe a fall in the magnitude of the CR. In animals, however, which, before the drug, are not so close to the threshold of transmarginal inhibition, caffeine should actually increase the magnitude of the CR (because it increases the intensity of the excitatory process set up by the CS). Both kinds of observation were made in Pavlov's laboratory; and it was inferred that a dog in which caffeine causes a fall in the magnitude of the CR has a weak nervous system, and one in which the drug causes an increase in CR magnitude has a strong one. This way of using drugs to determine the physiological basis of individual differences has been extremely influential in the development of research on human personality, both in the Soviet Union and in the West.

These and other methods were developed to measure the strength of the nervous system in different individuals. Much of the work testing whether these methods all give the same answer has been done since Pavlov's death, and is therefore beyond the scope of this book. But it can be asserted with confidence that some such dimension of personality as the one Pavlov called 'the strength of the nervous system' exists in both animals and Man.

The second major property of the nervous system postulated by Pavlov was the balance or equilibrium between the excitatory and inhibitory processes. The fundamental notion here is that in some ('excitable') animals, the excitatory process is stronger than the inhibitory process; in some ('inhibitable'), the inhibitory process is stronger than the excitatory process; and in others ('balanced'), the two processes are more or less of equal strength. Excitable dogs form positive conditioned reflexes more readily than inhibitory ones; and, once the reflexes are formed, they perform a positive CR more efficiently than they inhibit it. Inhibitable dogs show the converse characteristics. This strand of Pavlov's thinking was later taken up by the British psychologist, H. J. Eysenck, and incorporated in his important theory of the biological basis of extraversion.

The idea of equilibrium was the first to be clearly formulated by Pavlov in his attempts to understand personality, though in these early speculations (around 1915) he tended in part to use the vocabulary which he later

pplied to the concept of strength of the nervous system.
hus, at this time, he would talk of a dog which had a
redominance of inhibition over excitation sometimes as
inhibitable' but sometimes as 'weak'. This is, of course,
very confusing when one attempts to put side by side ideas
that Pavlov expressed at different times in the development
of his theory of personality. It was only in the last years of
his life that the ideas of strength and equilibrium were
gradually separated from each other; and the process was
completed only by Pavlov's successors in the field of personality, B. M. Teplov and V. D. Nebylitsyn.

Pavlov's first ideas about excitable and inhibitable types
of animal came from observations of the general behaviour
of his dogs, not from special experiments. It was noticed
that some dogs were extremely lively and active when at
liberty, while others were calm and slow-moving. This
observation will hardly come as a surprise to anyone who
has ever watched dogs. What *was* surprising was that the
lively dogs proved difficult to work with in conditioning
experiments – not because they were over-active, but because they fell asleep immediately they were put in the
special harness used to keep them still. The dogs which
were tranquil while at liberty, in complete contrast, were
perfectly wide-awake in the conditioning experiments.

By this time, Pavlov had formulated his theory of excitation and inhibition as wave-like processes flowing through
the cerebral tissue. Furthermore, he had proposed that, as
he put it in the title of one of his articles, 'inhibition and
sleep are one and the same process'. By this he meant that,
if the inhibitory process spreads through the brain un-
checked by pockets of excitation, the whole brain enters a
state of lowered functioning, and this is seen behaviourally
as sleep. (This is not a view of sleep that is easily tenable
in the light of modern research.) Applying these ideas to
the curious behaviour of the dogs which were lively at
liberty, but fell asleep in the experimental stand, Pavlov
supposed them to be excessively susceptible to the spread

of inhibition (and therefore to sleep). Consider such a do
while it is at liberty. It will initially be exposed to som
stimulation or other. According to Pavlov, the cortical cell
thus stimulated rapidly enter into a state of inhibition an
this, by induction, produces a general excitation. This exc
tation, by impelling the dog to move to and fro, expose
other cells to new stimuli and thus, when the animal is a
liberty, a more extensive development and spread of inhibi
tion is prevented. But now put the dog in the experimenta
stand. Since it cannot move about, and is exposed to only
monotonous stimuli, there is nothing to limit the spread o
inhibition, so the animal falls rapidly asleep. (Connoisseur
of Eysenckian theory will at once recognize this as th
description of an extraverted dog.)

Such a dog, then, was thought to have a predominance o
inhibition over excitation. Later, more formal experimen
tal procedures were developed to test the balance betwee
excitation and inhibition. The most important of these wa
the comparative speed with which an animal formed, o
the one hand, a positive conditioned reflex and, on th
other, a differentiation. The logic of this test flows directly
from the basic idea of equilibrium as outlined above. Fo
example, as early as 1910 attention was drawn to th
difference between two dogs, one of which took 27 trials tc
form a CR and 70 to form a differentiation, while the othe
took 147 trials to form the CR and only 7 to form th
differentiation. Not surprisingly, the former dog was classi
fied as 'excitable', the latter as 'inhibitable'.

Pavlov tried out various other tests of the balance be
tween excitation and inhibition, and since his death othe
workers in the Soviet Union have taken up the problem
But so far progress in establishing a clear-cut dimension o
equilibrium has been much poorer than in the case o
strength of the nervous system. Much the same problem
has arisen in Western work based on Eysenck's suggestion
that extraverts form positive conditioned reflexes less well
but inhibitory reflexes better, than introverts. So far, it has

een impossible to demonstrate consistent individual differ-
nces in conditionability which extend across more than
ne or two closely related tasks. As soon as radically
ifferent UCSs or even CSs are used, it becomes impossible
o predict from the ease of either positive or inhibitory
onditioning in one task to the ease of conditioning in a
econd.

The third property of the nervous system, 'mobility', was
ot postulated until the last years of Pavlov's life. Thus it
an be regarded only as a suggestion for future work. The
asic notion is that the nervous processes, both excitatory
nd inhibitory, may move (and we have seen that they are
iven a lot of moving to do in Pavlov's theory) with more
r less rapidity. The more mobile the nervous processes, the
aster (Pavlov thought) the nervous process is initiated,
evelops, irradiates, concentrates and comes to an end; and
lso, if the animal is stimulated at a short interval by two
timuli, one positive and one negative, the faster is excita-
ion replaced by inhibition or vice versa. Thus the concept
f mobility is an extremely broad one. Unfortunately, Pav-
ov did not have time to pin it down to particular experi-
nental operations before his death (though several methods
vere tried out); and so far attempts by other workers to
lemonstrate a unitary property of mobility have not met
vith much success. Nonetheless, the idea of mobility as a
ossible factor affecting individual differences continues to
nfluence contemporary research.

This, then, in outline, was Pavlov's theory of canine
ersonality at the time of his death. All dogs have the same
asic nervous processes, consisting of excitation plus a
umber of processes of inhibition which he counted
variously as three (internal, external and transmarginal) or
one, depending on the degree of optimism he felt at the
ime about the possibility of unifying them. The way in
which one dog differs from another can be attributed to
the strength of the cortical cells (enabling them to withstand an excitatory process of greater or lesser intensity);

to the degree to which excitation or inhibition predom
nates when the animal has to deal with both positive an
inhibitory conditioned stimuli; and to the speed with whic
these two nervous processes arise and move across th
brain. Different types of dog (in the sense of animals di
playing characteristically different patterns of behaviou
arise from different combinations of values along thes
three dimensions of strength, equilibrium and mobility c
the nervous processes.

If we take this theory of personality as a description c
the way in which differences in the functioning of the rea
brain affect differences in behaviour, then it must suffe
from the same criticisms as Pavlov's general theory of brai
function considered in the previous chapter. Taken as
conceptual nervous system, however, it has had and sti
has much to offer. From this point of view, the importan
question is, does the theory make testable and successfu
predictions about which kinds of individual differences g
together with which others? The subsequent work of Te
lov and Nebylitsyn in Moscow and Eysenck in London hav
made it clear that it does. Both these groups started off fron
Pavlov's theory of the personality of dogs and applied i
to Man. As new experiments have been performed and nev
data obtained, they have needed to modify and exten
Pavlov's ideas. Nonetheless, both Eysenck's theories an
those of Teplov and Nebylitsyn have remained recognizabl
Pavlovian; and both traditions of research have repeatedl
sought new impetus in Pavlov's original theories and ex
periments.

From personality to disordered personality is a smal
step; and a laboratory of individual differences is usuall
found close to the psychiatric clinic. For, if individuals ca
be ranked along a behavioural continuum, those at on
extreme or other are statistically rare and, often, psycho
logically abnormal as well. It was to be expected, therefore
that Pavlov should find himself drawn in the direction o

psychopathology (the study of disordered behaviour). This development was the more natural in that his two major personality dimensions, strength of the nervous system and equilibrium, both include explicit notions of behavioural breakdown: an individual with a weak nervous system is unable to cope with excessively strong stimulation; an excitable individual cannot deal with a situation in which there is a strong need to restrain behaviour; and an inhibitable individual cannot easily maintain a positive behavioural output when surrounded by inhibitory stimuli. There was, however, a second source of Pavlov's interest in psychopathology. Quite early on in his investigations of conditioned reflexes he had observed that simple, and seemingly innocuous, behavioural procedures are sometimes capable of producing profound disturbances in behaviour. These two horses – the predisposing personality and the environmental stress – have pulled most of modern psychiatry, but usually in opposite directions. It was characteristic of Pavlov that he made them pull together: his interest lay in the question, how does personality *combine* with stress to produce a particular form of behavioural breakdown?

Pavlov had no experience of psychiatry, nor indeed clinical experience of any kind. To nourish his burgeoning interest in psychopathology, he began to visit psychiatric wards several times a week, and discuss the cases there with the incumbent psychiatrists. Thus did he set out on a new career of study and research – at the age of eighty! Gantt writes of a visit he paid to Pavlov during this period, 'I found him aglow from the visit of Adolf Meyer, the dean of American psychiatry at that time; and his desk was covered with the current texts of psychiatry in English, German and French.' (G II, p. 12.) Actually, the transition from the experimental laboratory to the psychiatric ward round was probably quite smooth; for Pavlov's regular laboratory seminars, in which week by week the personality and conditioning performance of each dog were minutely scrutinized, discussed and interpreted, read very much like clinical case conferences.

Indeed, the transition from laboratory to clinic was too smooth; for Pavlov talked of schizophrenics, neurotics and hysterics rather as if they were dogs whose conditioning performance had gone wrong, and offered much the same kinds of explanation in the two cases. And even the most ardent supporter of the view that humans and other animals differ only in degree, not kind, is likely to find this approach simplistic. Thus most of Pavlov's specific suggestions about the aetiology of mental illness already seem historical curiosities. Rather too many illnesses which are radically different from one another were attributed to the same disturbance in conditioning or brain function. Both hysteria and schizophrenia, for example, were said to result from the generation of transmarginal inhibition in an excessively weak nervous system, although they are undoubtedly distinct syndromes from the clinical point of view. In other cases the explanations offered for the genesis of such symptoms as obsessions or paranoid delusions are too strained to carry conviction. These explanations, however, have little to do with Pavlov's importance for psychopathology. This, as so often with Pavlov, is to be found in his experimental method: for the first time, he brought disturbed behaviour under experimental control.

The first observations of disturbed behaviour during conditioning experiments were incidental to other research. In the earliest of these experiments (by Yerofeyeva in 1912) an electric shock to the skin was used as a CS for food. So long as the shock was applied to one part of the dog's body only, the original reactions to it (attempts to escape and to bite the apparatus) were eliminated completely and replaced by a conditioned salivary response. (This observation is known as 'counter-conditioning', and is itself one of the most important to come from Pavlov's laboratory; we shall return to it later.) But when the shock was applied to parts of the dog's body other than those at which the initial training had taken place, not only was there no generalization of the salivary response, but the established conditioned reflexes disappeared and it was then very difficult to restore them by further training. At the same time, the animal became very excited.

These observations are not particularly surprising, given that Yerofeyeva used a painful CS. But it turned out later that the same kind of behavioural disturbance can be produced using nothing more sinister than food and ordinary conditioned stimuli. In a famous experiment by Shenger-Krestovnika, published in 1921, a dog was trained to salivate to a circle but not to an ellipse. The ellipse was now progressively made more like a circle. When the ratio of the axes of the ellipse was reduced to 9 : 8, the dog could discriminate it from a circle only with great difficulty. It showed some signs of success on this problem for about three weeks, but then its behaviour was totally disrupted. It was quite unable to respond correctly not only on this difficult task, but also when presented with perfectly obvious ellipses and circles which had given it no trouble in the earlier part of the experiment. What is more, instead of coming to stand quietly in the apparatus as in the past, the animal now showed extreme excitement, struggling and howling.

Pavlov interpreted this breakdown in the dog's performance as being due to a 'collision' between the excitatory and inhibitory processes. Given his theories about the movement of the nervous processes across the tissue of the brain, he meant this as more than a metaphor. One not committed to a Pavlovian view of brain function would probably say that Shenger-Krestovnika's experiment produced a conflict between a tendency to respond (Pavlov's excitatory process) and a tendency not to respond (the inhibitory process). The remarkable thing is that this conflict, involving as it does no painful or threatening stimuli, should give rise to such a profound disturbance in behaviour. Other methods, super-

ficially equally innocuous, proved to have similar effects:
presenting a CS+ very rapidly after a CS−; prolonging the
period of action of an inhibitory stimulus; and irregular
reinforcement of the same CS, sometimes following it with
the UCS, sometimes not.

In these and other ways, then, Pavlov learned how to
create an 'experimental neurosis', as he put it in a phrase
which has since stuck. The work on experimental neurosis
proceeded hand in hand with that on the different types of
dog. And one of the most important aspects of Pavlov's
work in this field is that he showed how the same treatment produced different kinds of breakdown in different
animals, depending on their personalities. Petrova, for example, made use of Yerofeyeva's technique in which an
electric shock is used as the CS for a salivary CR. She used
two animals, one excitable, the other inhibitable. With
both dogs Petrova had previously established a number of
other conditioned reflexes, differentiations, delayed reflexes and so on. The new CR to the electric shock CS was
successfully set up. But when the shock CS was delivered
several times in succession the behaviour of both animals
broke down, but in different ways. In the case of the excitable dog, the established positive CSs continued to act normally, but the erstwhile inhibitory stimuli now came also
to elicit positive responses. In the case of the inhibitable
dog, exactly the opposite took place: the inhibitory stimuli
continued to act normally but the positive CSs ceased
eliciting any response. This experiment is an excellent
demonstration of the need to take into account *both* environmental stress *and* the predisposing personality, if one
is successfully to predict behaviour.

After illness there should come therapy. As long ago as
1899, while still working on the digestive system, Pavlov
had written that 'no one can say that he fully comprehends
the physiology of an organ till he is able to restore its
disordered function to a normal state. Hence, experimental
therapeutics is essentially a test of physiology.' (*WDG*, p.

243.) He had intended to develop his research on the digestive system along these lines, but, as we know, his interest turned to conditioned reflexes instead. A quarter of a century later, he returned to the strategy he had outlined in 1899, but now the object of therapy was the experimental neurosis.

Surprisingly, Pavlov's contribution to the therapeutics of neurosis was unimaginative; surprisingly because, in the principle of counter-conditioning seen in Yerofeyeva's experiment, he already had in his hands the tool which was later to fashion what is now known as 'behaviour therapy'. For once, however, this physiologist, whose response to nearly every previous problem had taken a behavioural form, had recourse to physiology. His remedy for all the ills that his cunning behavioural experiments could produce was – bromide; and, when not bromide, it was rest and prolonged sleep. Bromide was supposed to strengthen the inhibitory process. The rationale behind sleep therapy was no more compelling: 'experimental affections of the nervous system are almost invariably characterized by symptoms of hypnosis, which gives reason to suppose that this is a normal physiological means of struggling against a morbific agent.' (*G* II, p. 182.) I do not know what has happened to bromide, though it was once the physician's favourite remedy for most things. As for sleep therapy, Pavlov's recommendation made it very popular in the Soviet Union, but it has been little used elsewhere. It cannot be said, therefore, that Pavlov's direct contribution to the therapy of the neuroses amounted to much. But, as we shall see in the final chapter, his indirect contribution has been of the utmost importance.

7. Pavlov's Influence

Pavlov's materialist approach to the problems of mind and behaviour was congenial to the Bolshevik regime which came to power in Russia in 1918. Very shortly after the Revolution, when life in Russia was in a state of chaos, the new Soviet authorities began to extend quite exceptional advantages to his laboratories. A decree of 1921, signed by Lenin himself, set up a special committee to 'create as soon as possible the most favourable conditions for safeguarding the scientific work of Academician Pavlov and his collaborators'. The same decree even directed the Committee of Provisions for Workers to supply Academician Pavlov and his wife with double food rations.

Relations between Pavlov and the Soviet State were not, however, untroubled. At the personal level, Pavlov, a moderate liberal by political inclination, remained hostile to the new regime for many years, in spite of his extra rations. At the philosophical level, Pavlov's thorough-going materialism proved *too* radical for the subtle Marxist-Leninist dialectic that the Revolution brought in its wake. This dialectic recognizes two enemies, one to the left and one to the right. To the left there is 'mechanism' or 'vulgar materialism', which seeks to reduce all phenomena to the inevitable working out of the laws of physics and chemistry; to the right there is 'idealism', which allows the existence of a non-material medium in which mental events take place. To the Marxist-Leninist himself consciousness is a 'property of highly organized matter', not fully reducible to the laws of physics and chemistry, yet remaining a material process. During the 1920s and 1930s a fierce debate raged among psychologists, philosophers and Party officials (for nothing in the Soviet state is without political significance) as to the correct basis on which to build a Marxist psychology. Pavlov's theory of conditioned reflexes was one of the candidates. But it was rejected as being a variant of vulgar materialism – as, indeed, it is : for Pavlov, as we have seen, held that the explanation of behaviour and of mind consists simply in a description of the brain processes which bring about behaviour; and these, in turn, can be explained by physico-chemical laws.

By 1936 Pavlov's theory, as a basis for the general development of psychology, had been rejected by the Communist theocracy (though he and his work continued to be held in the highest esteem until his death in that year). Conditioning theory was in good company, however, for every other theory which had been proposed as a possible basis for a Marxist psychology had also been rejected. From then until the end of the Second World War psychology ceased to have any official existence in the Soviet Union; although research on conditioned reflexes continued in many laboratories which had been founded by Pavlov's pupils throughout the country. After the war the Party began to look around again for a psychology befitting the 'new Soviet Man' that it was busy creating. In 1950 there was a special conference called by the Soviet Academy of Sciences to discuss this problem. As a result Pavlov was canonized. Dialectical possibilities which had passed unnoticed in the debates of earlier years were now discovered in his work, and it was declared that Pavlovian theory should in future provide the focus around which scientific research on higher nervous activity and psychology should revolve.

Pavlov's influence on those closest to him would in any circumstances have been a dominating one. In the hothouse of Soviet life, in which scientific error could easily become political deviation, it became a stultifying one. Konorski, who had first-hand experience, has commented on the way in which Pavlov's successors too often treated his theories as the revealed truth which, applied *post hoc*, explained everything. Thus the forty years which have passed since Pavlov's death have seen the accumulation of much new experimental material in the Soviet Union, but little development or critical evaluation of his theories. There are, of course, exceptions to this rule. Workers like Anokhin, Asratyan and Simonov have made important observations and modifications to Pavlovian theory; and Sokolov's work on the orienting reflex, which turned an almost incidental observation of Pavlov's into a whole new field of research, for the first time opened up the crucial problem of attention to experimental attack. But, reading Soviet papers published even in the 1970s, one all too often has the impression that time has stood still since 1936, and that nothing has changed in the world of conditioned reflexes since Pavlov's death.

Outside the Soviet Union Pavlov's influence has gone through several phases.

At first, it was largely symbolic, providing an experimentally based vocabulary for a revolution in thought that was bound to occur anyway. That revolution was known as behaviourism. The early behaviourists, led by Watson, took from Pavlov the language of conditioned reflexes, but not his methods or theories. Access to the details of his work was in any case limited until the large-scale translations of his papers into English published in 1927 and 1928. By this time the mould was set, and America (by now the heartland of psychology) continued to talk conditioned reflexes, but do other things, for several decades. The confusion was worse confounded by the lack of a clear distinction between classical and instrumental conditioning (see Chapter 4). This distinction did not become clear until the 1950s, though it was pointed out earlier by both Konorski and Skinner.

By that time, the second phase of Pavlov's influence in America had come and gone. This phase was dominated by the attempt of Clark Hull (1884–1952) to construct a completely general, mathematically formulated theory of learning. For this purpose, he drew freely on Pavlov's data, and also took over many of Pavlov's concepts (stripped, however, of their connections with the brain). But still, apart from a few isolated laboratories, there was little attempt actually to apply Pavlovian methods to the study of animal behaviour. Instead, the indigenous tradition of Thorndike flourished, and innumerable rats learned to run in mazes and pigeons to peck in boxes.

The third phase belongs to the 1950s and 1960s. With the distinction between classical and instrumental conditioning now widely accepted (though it is still today a matter of debate whether this is merely procedural or of fundamental significance to the learning process), there came the construction of so-called 'two-process' or 'two-factor' theories (by, for example, Mowrer, Amsel and Solomon). These theories suppose that classical conditioning is the process which underlies an animal's ability to learn the significance of the events in its environment, while instrumental conditioning provides the opportunity to learn to do something about them. It took fifteen years of such theorizing, in which a postulated classical conditioning process was called in to account for everything that was otherwise inexplicable, before American experimental psychologists at last began actually to study classical conditioning in the laboratory.

Thus, in this fourth phase (which we are still in today) a vigorous new experimental attack is being mounted on all the questions which Pavlov raised over fifty years ago. Observations which he reported in one or two experiments are being repeated with new techniques and a new rigour. His concepts are being given a critical scrutiny as never before (except by Konorski), and they are being pitted against a variety of alternative accounts of the same data. Thus the influence of Pavlov on the study of animal learning is stronger and more direct now than at any time in the past, and it appears still to be growing.

There is much, then, that Pavlov would find familiar if

he were able to visit an American or English laboratory where animal learning is studied today. He would recognize the questions asked, and the basic methods used to answer these questions. What would surprise and distress him is the separation between the study of conditioned reflexes and the study of the brain. For him these two branches of science were indissoluble. But today the psychologists, such as Rescorla, Wagner or Mackintosh, who study classical conditioning have little or nothing to do with the brain; and scientists who study the brain have equally little interest in conditioning.

Pavlov's own attempt to knit the two together in his theory of brain function was a failure. It has looked increasingly like a museum piece as we have come to know more about the actual functioning of the brain. Only occasionally has the new knowledge in this field looked as though it fits Pavlovian principles. There was a time, at the start of the 1960s, when it seemed that application of the technique of electroencephalography (EEG) to slow electrical rhythms in the brain might reveal processes corresponding to Pavlov's concepts of the irradiation and concentration of excitation and inhibition. But little of substance has emerged to justify these hopes. It seems unlikely that future research along these lines will fare better. What we need, rather, is a new synthesis between modern ideas of brain function and the behavioural principles that Pavlov discovered.

The most ambitious attempt to date to provide such a synthesis has been made by Konorski, in two important books. From his centrally placed listening post in Warsaw, Konorski could not fail to observe the enormous discrepancy between Pavlov's theory and the ideas of Sherrington on the reflex arc, ideas which, by the time the twentieth century was a couple of decades old, dominated the approach of Western physiologists to the nervous system. Thus, in his 1948 book, *Conditioned Reflexes and Neuron Organization*, Konorski made a detailed criticism of Pavlov's theory from a Sherringtonian point of view; and a valiant attempt to synthesize the two approaches into a new theory by reinterpreting Pavlov's observations in terms of the principles of reflex action established in the spinal cord. Konorski's 1948 theory was itself substantially modified and extended in his 1967 book, *Integrative Activity of the Brain*. It is too soon to judge the success of this theory, which is extremely wide-ranging, covering all that Pavlov covered and still more. Many of the ideas it contains have influenced theoretical developments in American psychology. But, outside Konorski's native Poland, his theory has failed so far to stimulate much new research directed to those crucial Pavlovian questions: how does the brain produce, modify and inhibit conditioned reflexes?

It is difficult to see how progress can be made in answering these questions so long as the brain and conditioning are studied in separate laboratories. No doubt this is a temporary separation rather than a complete divorce; and, when the right technique or theory is developed, the two parts of Pavlov's field of study will come together again. But for the moment we are no closer to understanding how the brain forms a conditioned reflex than was Pavlov; and very little is being done to improve this state of affairs.

We have seen that in the study of learning, the influence of Pavlov, after a number of vicissitudes, has now reached its apogee. A rather similar evolution has also taken place in the field of personality. Here too we can distinguish an earlier period of relatively indirect influence from a recent one in which Pavlovian ideas have more immediately affected the course of research. And here too Pavlov's influence is more widely felt now than ever before.

The period of indirect Pavlovian influence is dominated by the work of Hans Eysenck, at the Institute of Psychiatry in London. Eysenck approached personality from a quite different starting point from Pavlov's. Using the answers to questionnaires and subjecting them to complex mathematical analysis, he began with a careful description of the main ways in which human beings differ from each other. From this research he derived his well-known theory that individual differences can be accounted for in terms of only a very few major axes of variation ('dimensions of personality'), of which the principal ones are introversion-extraversion, neuroticism, psychoticism and intelligence. This part of Eysenck's research shows no trace of Pavlov's influence. It is in his attempt to explain the biological causes of these axes of variation that he draws heavily on Pavlovian ideas. In his 1957 book, *The Dynamics of Anxiety and Hysteria*, Eysenck proposed a theory of introversion-extraversion which, in effect, treats this as Pavlov's dimension of equilibrium between excitation and inhibition. According to this theory an introvert has a predominance of excitation over inhibition, and an extravert a predominance of inhibition over excitation. From this fundamental postulate a wide variety of experimental predictions were derived. Some of these Pavlov would at once have recognized (for example, that introverts should form conditioned reflexes better than extraverts); others would have baffled him, since they depend on an extension of his concepts of excitation and inhibition into domains of psychological research which bear very little resemblance to conditioned reflexes.

A vast amount of research was stimulated by this theory, as documented in the many books Eysenck has written since 1957. A decade later, it was clear that, in its original form, the theory would not work, and Eysenck proposed a second theory, similar in many respects to the first, but also with substantial changes, in *The Biological Basis of Personality* (1967). The Pavlovian influence was equally strong in this second theory, but it now took a different form. The change was at least in part due to the fact that it had now become possible to form a much clearer idea of the details of Pavlov's own theory of personality. For, in the interim, the work of Teplov's group in Moscow had become known in the West.

As we saw earlier in this chapter, it was officially declared in 1950 that psychology in the Soviet Union must
go Pavlovian. This official directive ought to have ensured
that nothing good would come out of psychology until the
directive had been forgotten; for 'official' science, like
'official' art, nearly always lacks either quality or inspiration. To this rule, Teplov's work stands as a glowing excep-
tion. He did just what the Party ordered, and constructed
personality theory on a Pavlovian basis; but he did it
superlatively well and with great originality.

As a start Teplov performed a careful analysis of Pavlov's
own ideas on personality. As pointed out in the last chapter, these ideas underwent constant modification throughout the quarter of a century that Pavlov puzzled over the
differences between his dogs. It is therefore all too easy to
juxtapose concepts proposed at different times during this
intellectual evolution and come up with nonsense. In a
scholarly dissection of the different stages of Pavlov's
developing thought, Teplov brought out clearly the various
hypotheses which might serve as the basis for a theory
applicable to human personality. He and his colleagues then
set about devising new experimental methods which could
be used with human subjects to test these hypotheses. As
was to be expected, not all of Pavlov's ideas survived this
new and critical evaluation. But some of them did, and
with flying colours; these were incorporated by Teplov, and
later by Nebylitsyn, into an important new theory of the
biological basis of human personality.

The work of the Moscow group has influenced Western
research on personality in three ways. First, Teplov's
analysis of the development of Pavlov's ideas, available in
English since 1964, made a just appreciation of Pavlovian
personality theory possible for the first time. As a result,
this theory is now much more widely known in English
and American laboratories. Second, the experimental work
carried out in Moscow, besides having a great impact in its
own right, clearly demonstrated that many of Pavlov's

ideas are applicable to human beings. Finally, a number of important ideas developed by Pavlov, Teplov and Nebylitsyn, most notably those concerned with the strength of the nervous system, were incorporated by Eysenck in his 1967 theory of the biological basis of introversion-extraversion. Since Eysenck's theories continue to inspire a veritable flood of research, this last route is of particular importance. The net result is that, today, virtually all serious research on the biological basis of personality can be traced in one way or another to ideas first advanced by Pavlov.

Thus Pavlov's influence is today pervasive in laboratories where one studies learning or personality. That is, no doubt, of interest to practitioners of these obscure pursuits, but the average citizen does not often enter such places. Where will *he* find Pavlov's influence? Most practically, if he is unfortunate enough to need to go there, in the psychiatric clinic.

We saw in the last chapter that Pavlov's own attempts to treat neurosis centred on the use of drugs. Treatment of psychiatric disorders in this way has greatly expanded since Pavlov's day, especially with the discovery of anti-depressant and anti-anxiety drugs. But Pavlov's work had nothing to do with these developments. It is in the development of behavioural methods of treatment that we must look for his influence.

These methods have evolved rapidly during the last twenty-five years, and now constitute the most effective form of therapy for the majority of common neurotic ailments (phobias, obsessional rituals, anxiety states etc.). One of the most widely used techniques is known as 'desensitisation'. The principle on which it is based is essentially that of counter-conditioning, discovered in Pavlov's laboratory by Yerofeyeva. As we saw in the previous chapter, by using an electric shock as the CS for food, Yerofeyeva was able to convert the normal reaction to shock (pain, withdrawal etc.) into a conditioned salivary response. In desensitisation therapy, much the same thing is done. The patient is presented with a stimulus which evokes an unpleasant reaction (for example, if the patient has a phobia of cats, a picture of a cat might be used), and this is followed by a second stimulus (acting as a UCS) which evokes a pleasant reaction. With repeated pairings of the two stimuli, it is possible to weaken the phobic response and replace it with the pleasant feelings evoked by the UCS. In this way the phobia is eliminated.

Many variants on this basic principle have been devised by clinical psychologists faced with a diversity of behavioural problems. The 'stimulus' used as the CS, for example, may be an instruction to imagine a scene which produces anxiety; and the UCS may be nothing more than the therapist saying 'well done' or telling the subject to relax. Or the whole procedure may be reversed and used to eliminate a habit which the patient finds pleasant but which is harmful on other grounds (smoking, for example, or dressing up in the clothing of the opposite sex, may be followed by an electric shock). But the principle remains recognizably Pavlovian, and it is remarkably effective across this diversity of specific procedures.

It would be wrong to say that these methods have replaced the ineffective methods spawned by psycho-analysis and its congeners; but that it is only because psycho-analysis takes so long and costs so much that the great majority of people who now benefit from behaviour therapy would not previously have received any treatment at all. Behaviour therapy, in contrast, is cheap and quick, as well as effective. It is in providing the basis for this method of treatment that Pavlov has had the most direct impact on modern life. And it is likely that this impact will grow, for the methods of behaviour therapy are year by year coming into wider use.

Not everyone, however, welcomes these clinical successes. For some the notion that the principles of conditioning, derived from the study of animals, can be used to alter and control human behaviour is a threat to their most cherished beliefs about the nature of Man. The term 'reflex', whether conditioned or not, calls forth the image of a slot machine, or of the mechanical toys which first inspired Descartes' mechanistic theories of the behaviour of animals: insert an appropriate stimulus and the corresponding response fatally occurs. But there is much in common experience that this image fits ill, if at all. We all know what it is to think about what to do, solve a problem, make a decision and so on. This kind of behaviour not only does not feel like a reflex, it is precisely in opposition to it that we recognize *as* reflex a blink of the eye or a sneeze in sudden sunlight. Tell us that both kinds of behaviour are reflex, and we feel puzzled. And, if we believe that there is a non-material world to which mind gives access, a world perhaps charged with spiritual significance, the puzzle may become outrage or panic. Here, for example, is Bernard Shaw's reaction to Pavlov's work:

... it denies not only the existence and authority of Jehovah but of any metaphysical factors in life whatsoever, including purpose, intuition, inspiration, and all the religious and artistic impulses. It boycotts volition, conscience, and even consciousness as unaccounted for in science. In short, it seeks to abolish life and mind, substituting for them a conception of all motion and action, bodily and mental, as a senseless accidental turmoil of physical collisions.

(*Everybody's Political What's What*, p. 203.)

There are several levels at which this kind of charge against Pavlov (and Shaw's diatribe goes on for many more pages) can be understood and combatted.

At the most primitive level it is a protest against any kind of scientific attempt to understand the workings of the mind. From this point of view it is essential to preserve a mystery about consciousness, conscience, volition and the like, so that one can conjecture 'through a glass darkly' whatever glamorous or awe-inspiring metaphysics one finds most satisfying. There is little one can say in rebuttal of such an attitude. It is largely a matter of taste whether one prefers a satisfying image of Man or the truth, insofar as we can establish it, about how he actually works. But, in the long run, it is difficult to see how any image which is radically different from the truth can survive. At the very least, it will be a poor guide to action in a world in which the decisions real men take have increasingly dangerous effects.

At a more sophisticated level, one can accept that the attempt to understand the workings of the mind is legitimate, but claim that all such attempts so far, if they have started from the assumption of physico-chemical determinacy, have been failures. From this conclusion it may be inferred that mind requires for its understanding some further principles which lie outside the normal scientific laws governing the behaviour of material systems. This is a position which has been adopted by eminent men of science who have themselves carried out extensive investigations of the brain, Sir John Eccles being perhaps the most famous example. It suffers, however, from a major flaw. It is a position which can be established only by default. Since we have no way of independently investigating the non-material principles which, it is alleged, enter into the realm of mind, all we can do is try to push the normal materialist principles of science as far as they can go, registering failure when we must. And it would be premature, less than a century after serious scientific research into the brain and behaviour has begun, to announce irreversible defeat.

There is a third level, however, at which the Shavian reaction to Pavlov is better justified. At this level, the protest is against an illegitimate extension of the concept of reflex. The feeling that there is a fundamental difference between the purposive behaviour I display in writing this book and an involuntary eye-blink is soundly based. This is not to say that the one is the product of spiritual forces and the other part of the physical world. Both are products of the activity of that physical system which is the brain; but they are surely products of a different order of complexity, and to call them both 'reflex' obscures rather than illuminates this difference. *This* charge against Pavlov deserves careful examination.

In fact, as we saw in Chapter 1, the concept of reflex action had been widening its scope for half a century before Pavlov began his work on conditioned reflexes. In the controversy over spinal reflexes Pflüger had treated purposiveness as a criterion by which one could recognize those more-than-reflex factors which, at that time, were still talked of as signs of 'soul'. Only a few years later Sechenov turned Pflüger's argument on its head and treated purposiveness as the veritable hall-mark of reflex action. And there can be little doubt that Sechenov's move is descriptively correct: what is there more purposeful than the reflex movement by which the hand is withdrawn from the flame, an example already used in the seventeenth century by Descartes?

If reflexes are purposive, purpose cannot be used to distinguish reflex from non-reflex action. The next move tried during the nineteenth century was Lotze's proposal that reflexes cannot adapt to changed circumstances: only consciousness can do this. In effect, Pavlov's work was a massive answer to Lotze. The conditioned reflex is nothing if not adaptation to a changing environment. But is it a *reflex*? Is it, say, the same sort of thing as the jerk of the knee which follows a tap on the patellar tendon?

At one level we shall only be able to answer this question when we have fully understood the neural machinery which controls both kinds of reaction, conditioned and unconditioned reflexes; when we have dealt, in fact, with all the problems which we noted as still outstanding in Chapters 4 and 5. But a little thought shows that the conditioned reflex is, indeed, for the purpose of the present argument, a reflex. If there is a distinction between knee-jerks and book-writing, the conditioned salivary response is on the knee-jerk side of the divide, not that of the writing of books. When my mouth waters at the sight of my favourite dish, or even at the thought of it, I do not ponder whether or not to salivate, I just salivate. It is for this reason that conditioning techniques are so successful when applied to neurotic behaviour. For the hall-mark of this kind of behaviour is that the patient *cannot deliberately do anything about it*. He knows that it is absurd to fear a cat, but the fear comes anyway. That is why he needs therapy.

Pavlov, then, was justified in aligning the conditioned reflex with the spinal reflexes described in the previous century. Certainly, there must be important differences in the detailed machinery by which the two kinds of reflex work; and Pavlov spent much of his scientific life attempting to discover those differences. But the conditioned reflex does not require consciousness or volition, any more than the unconditioned. So adaptation to change, the *raison d'être* of the conditioned reflex, is of no more value than purposiveness as a criterion of mind or soul.

And yet the intuition remains. In what does the distinction between reflex and non-reflex action (if it exists) consist? To this question we have, at present, no answer; for we do not yet know enough about how (apparently) non-reflex behaviour is organized and controlled. Pavlov's research, important as it has been, ceases at this point to offer us any clues. Indeed, it managed for some time to obscure the nature of the problem, and even its existence. It is in this respect that the Shavian cry of outrage contains a legitimate criticism.

Pavlov's mistake was not that he over-extended the concept of the reflex by applying it to conditioning; it was rather that he over-extended the concept of the conditioned reflex by applying it indiscriminately to all behaviour. Two examples will serve to illustrate this point.

In 1916 Pavlov devoted a whole lecture, almost lyrical in tone, to what he called 'the reflex of purpose'. (*G* I, p. 275.) Under this heading he grouped behaviour as diverse as the simple grasp reflex, the gathering of food and the collection of money or stamps. No experimental or other empirical evidence was offered in support of this grouping together of different activities; nor any in support of their treatment as all 'reflex' in the way that the grasp reflex undoubtedly is. Worse still, the phrase 'reflex of purpose' begs the crucial question of mechanism: the mechanism by which an absent goal is able to control behaviour directed towards itself. We know today that the principles of classical conditioning are unlikely by themselves to be able to account for such goal-directed behaviour; although other principles, no less mechanistic, probably can. That is one reason why, within the theory of learning, it has become necessary to distinguish between Pavlovian conditioning and instrumental learning (see Chapter 4). Thus for Pavlov to talk about a 'reflex of purpose' in this way was empirically empty, expressive only of an attitude of mind.

The second example concerns language. In a phrase which has since been widely used by self-professed Pavlovians, Pavlov described language as a 'second signalling system', the set of conditioned stimuli constituting the first. Man shares with other animals the first signalling system. But the second is exclusively his. It consists of signals of the first signals, i.e. signals of ordinary conditioned stimuli. Possession of the second signalling system, according to Pavlov, allows Man to regulate his own behaviour to a degree not possible in the rest of the animal kingdom.

These statements were seized upon when, in 1950, it was decided to bless Pavlov as an acceptable Marxist cornerstone for psychology. Since the second signalling system, like the first, is a product of the brain, it is sufficiently materialist for dialectical materialism. But, at the same time, it provides a plausible scientific basis for some of the other tenets of Marxist-Leninism. It can easily be wedded to the Leninist doctrine of 'reflection', according to which truth is the reflection in the human brain of the actual objects and causal connections which exist in the world outside us; for, if words are signals of signals of unconditioned stimuli, they provide an accurate route for the formation of this 'reflection'. In addition, the concept of the second signalling system bolsters the distinction between Man and the animals, a distinction which Marxist-Leninism likes to stress almost as much as does Catholicism; yet it offers no loop-holes for the re-creation of the immortal soul. Finally, by emphasizing the regulatory role of the second signalling system, the Party theorist is able to find a scientific parallel for the Marxist doctrine that consciousness actively controls behaviour.

And so, after thirty years, the Soviet state had found a satisfactory solution to the problem of establishing a Marxist theory of psychology. But this solution, like the reflex of purpose, is purely verbal. Pavlov does not tell us what testable predictions about language we are to derive from its description as a 'second signalling system'; nor do any of his successors. We know nothing more about language after we have applied this description than we knew before. It is undoubtedly true that words can function as conditioned stimuli. This has been demonstrated frequently in the laboratory; and the contemporary industry of pornography offers massive testimony to the power of the conditioned reflexes that words evoke. But to treat language as *merely* a set of conditioned reflexes hardly does justice to its use, say, in the framing of a contract or a scientific theory. Once again, the real problems posed by the existence of language are swept under the carpet by an illegitimate extension of the concept of the conditioned reflex; and it is of no avail to talk of signals of signals rather than signals of unconditioned stimuli.

Why, then, did Pavlov talk in this way? No doubt, in large part, it was the desire, common enough among scientists, to extend a favourite theory as far as it can go. But there was, I think, a second reason. Talk about reflexes was, at the time Pavlov wrote, inextricably linked with the general attempt to provide a materialist account of mind and behaviour. If one wanted to say, as Sechenov did and Pavlov after him, that men are machines, there was virtually no other way of saying it except in the language of reflexes. Nowadays we have other examples of machines, more complex than the mechanical toys which inspired Descartes. We have, above all, those very intelligent machines called computers; and we have theories of cybernetics and control engineering which enable us to describe with precision mechanisms and processes which do not fit at all well with the language of reflexes. We can, therefore, say of a piece of behaviour that it is *not* reflex without implying that it is not the product of physico-chemical processes amenable to normal scientific investigation. Pavlov had no easy way of making this distinction. It is for this reason, I believe, that he felt impelled to talk of all behaviour as though it fitted the reflex and conditioned-reflex model.

Today no one is likely to try to account for language in terms of conditioned reflexes. But most scientists take it for granted that this kind of behaviour, like any other, is in some way due to the workings of the brain, and that the brain is a physico-chemical system, not different in principle from other such systems. This point of view is almost as common among people who have no professional interest in either brain or behaviour. That this is so is in no small measure due to the impact that Pavlov's theories and experiments have had on our twentieth-century image of Man.

Short Bibliography

The letters in brackets are abbreviations used in the text.

Works by Pavlov

The Work of the Digestive Glands, translated by W. H. Thompson, London, Griffin, 1902 (*WDG*).

Conditioned Reflexes: An Investigation of the Physiological Activity of the Cerebral Cortex, translated and edited by G. V. Anrep, Oxford University Press, 1927 (*A*).

Lectures on Conditioned Reflexes, Volume I : *Twenty-five Years of Objective Study of the Higher Activity (Behaviour) of Animals*, translated and edited by W. H. Gantt, New York, International Publishers, 1928 (*G I*).

Lectures on Conditioned Reflexes, Volume II : *Conditioned Reflexes and Psychiatry*, translated and edited by W. H. Gantt, London, Lawrence and Wishart, 1941 (*G II*).

Lectures on Conditioned Reflexes, single-volume edition, translated and edited by W. H. Gantt with new introduction by J. A. Gray, London, Julian Friedmann Publishers, 1979.

Selected Works, translated by S. Belsky, Moscow, Foreign Languages Publishing House, 1955.

Other relevant works

B. P. Babkin, *Pavlov, a Biography*, University of Chicago Press, 1949 (*B*).

J. A. Gray (editor), *Pavlov's Typology*, Oxford, Pergamon Press, 1964.

J. A. Gray, *Elements of a Two-Process Theory of Learning*, London, Academic Press, 1975.

Pavlov

R. A. Gregory, *Secretory Mechanisms of the Gastro-Intestinal Tract*, London, Arnold, 1962.

J. Konorski, *Conditioned Reflexes and Neuron Organisation*, Cambridge University Press, 1948.

N. J. Mackintosh, *The Psychology of Animal Learning*, London, Academic Press, 1974.

For kind permission to redraw and publish the figures in this book, thanks are due to Oxford University Press (for Figure 1, which is based on a photograph reproduced in E. G. T. Liddell, *The Discovery of Reflexes*, 1960; the original and its description first appeared in 1865 in a monograph by the German physiologist, O. Deiters); Academic Press and N. J. Mackintosh (for Figures 2 and 3, from N. Mackintosh, *The Psychology of Animal Learning*, © Academic Press Inc. (London) Ltd, 1974); and Cambridge University Press (for Figure 4, from J. Konorski, *Conditioned Reflexes and Neuron Organisation*, 1948).